KV-270-512

Developing Personal Potential

Chartered Management Institute Open Learning Programme

OTHER BOOKS WITHIN THIS SERIES

DEVELOPING PERSONAL POTENTIAL

Second edition

Revised by: Corinne Leech

Series Editor: Kate Williams

chartered
management
institute

ELSEVIER

Pergamon
Flexible
Learning

AMSTERDAM • BOSTON • HEIDELBERG • LONDON • OXFORD • NEW YORK • PARIS •
SAN DIEGO • SAN FRANCISCO • SINGAPORE • SYDNEY • TOKYO

Elsevier
Linacre House, Jordan Hill, Oxford OX2 8DP
200 Wheeler Road, Burlington, MA 01803

First published 1997
Second edition 2004

Copyright © Chartered Management Institute, 1977. All rights reserved
Copyright © Elsevier Limited, 2004. All rights reserved

No part of this publication may be reproduced in any material form (including
photocopying or storing in any medium by electronic means and whether or not
transiently or incidentally to some other use of this publication) without the written permission of the copyright holder except in accordance with the provisions
of the Copyright, Designs and Patents Act 1988 or under the terms of a licence
issued by the Copyright Licensing Agency Ltd, 90 Tottenham Court Road, London,
England W1T 4LP. Applications for the copyright holder's written permission to
reproduce any part of this publication should be addressed to the publishers

Permissions may be sought directly from Elsevier's Science and Technology
Rights Department in Oxford, UK: phone: (+44) (0) 1865 843830; fax: (+44) (0)
1865 853333; e-mail: permissions@elsevier.co.uk. You may also complete
your request on-line via the Elsevier homepage (http://www.elsevier.com), by
selecting 'Customer Support' and then 'Obtaining Permissions'

British Library Cataloguing in Publication Data
A catalogue record for this book is available from the British Library

ISBN 0 7506 64231

For information on all Elsevier publications visit our website at
http://books.elsevier.com

Revised by: Corinne Leech
Editor: Kate Williams
Based on previous material in the Chartered Management Institute Opening
Learning Programme, 1997; Series Editor: Gareth Lewis.

Typeset by Charon Tec Pvt. Ltd, Chennai, India
Printed and bound in Italy

Contents

Series overview

The Chartered Management Institute Flexible Learning Programme is a series of workbooks prepared by the Chartered Management Institute and Elsevier for managers seeking to develop themselves.

Comprising ten open learning workbooks, the programme covers the best of modern management theory and practice. Each workbook provides a range of frameworks and techniques to improve your effectiveness as a manager, thus helping you acquire the knowledge and skill to make you fully competent in your role.

Each workbook is written by an experienced management writer and covers an important management topic or theme. The activities both reinforce learning and help to relate the generic ideas to your individual work context. While coverage of each topic is fully comprehensive, additional reading suggestions and reference sources are given for those who wish to study to a greater depth.

Designed to be practical, stimulating and challenging, the aim of the workbooks is to improve performance at work by benefiting you and your organization. This practical focus is at the heart of the competence-based approach that has been adopted by the programme.

Introduction

When people talk about 'the role of the manager' the focus is usually external and looks outwards from the person who is doing the managing. So there is much talk of managing resources, people, tasks and processes.

But efficient and effective management really begins 'at home'. In much the same way as we expect doctors to manage their own health – *'physician, heal thyself'* – most organizations expect their managers to be good at managing themselves. The thinking goes that if someone is a good self-manager, then he or she is more likely to be able to manage other people.

Managing yourself is very much about the skills of managing:

- your development, making sure you are continually learning and building on your experiences
- your self-confidence

- stress – which is also inevitable and arises out of the process of just getting on with your job and living your life
- time – which is a finite resource and which can be used effectively, but which can't be stretched (there are only 24 hours in a day and 7 days in each week, no matter how powerful or important you are)
- relationships – it's essential to have good working relationships with the people you work with
- conflict which arises at work, both between yourself and other people and between the members of your team.

In this workbook we are going to focus on these important self-management skills which will enable you to work more confidently, more efficiently and effectively.

Objectives

By the end of this Workbook you should be able to:

- identify any areas of personal or professional development you would like to work on
- apply techniques to ensure a positive, assertive approach
- understand the nature of stress and apply techniques for stress management
- effectively manage your time
- identify the foundations for good working relationships
- use a range of skills to deal with difficult people and manage different types of conflict situations.

Section 1   Personal development

Introduction

Personal development is an ongoing process which for many people, continues throughout life.

'Anyone who stops learning is old, whether at 2 or 80. Anyone who keeps learning stays young. The greatest thing in life is to keep your mind young.'

Moshe Arens (b. 1925)

We all develop and change as we grow older. It's an inevitable process and a result of life experiences. You have a choice; you can take charge of that development and influence it or you can sit back and let life take its own course. By selecting the option to take charge, you will be able to achieve your full potential and move towards the future you want for yourself.

The first section of this workbook is designed to help you think about what personal development means for you and how you can identify those areas where you would like to make changes or improvements.

What is personal development?

Personal development means different things to different people. Here is what a group of European managers said in response to the question, 'How would you define personal development?'

'It's about developing self-awareness. Personal development is the process of coming to understand yourself – knowing how you tick and what you do best.'

'I think personal development is about stretching yourself – not just in relation to the job, but in relation to every aspect of life. Relationships, money, health – everything.'

'It's about getting to be as good as you can be at what you want to do – so personal development relates to job skills, people skills, communication skills, I think.'

'Personal development for me, has always been about me expanding my horizons through travel and reading and meeting people. It's about being open to new ideas,

taking risks, being able to look at things in a new way. Whenever I feel I'm getting stuck in a rut I deliberately set myself a challenge. Last year it was learning to speak Spanish and this year I've taken up rock climbing. Every challenge helps me gain new skills but, most of all, gain confidence in myself and my abilities.'

'Personal development for me, is knowing more this year than I knew last year.'

'It's about knowing myself better – what I like, what I do well, what I'm capable of – and the arranging of my life to suit me.'

These responses all make it clear that personal development is different to career development. Career development is your 'job path'; the roles you take on in your working life. Personal development is about the way you evolve as a person. Inevitably the two are inextricably linked as you bring the behaviours and skills you develop as a person to your job role.

The following activity provides an opportunity for you to define what personal development means to you.

ACTIVITY 1

What does personal development mean to you in the context of your life, your goals and your ambitions? Take as long as you need to consider this question and then complete the sentence below.

For me, personal development is

FEEDBACK

There is no right or wrong answer to this question because everyone is different and has different interests, opinions, values and beliefs. Even so, for most people, personal development is about one or more of the following:

- developing greater self-awareness
- setting personal goals
- acquiring new skills and/or knowledge (which may or may not be job related).

The remainder of this section is designed to help you to examine each of these areas within your own life.

Developing greater self-awareness

Developing self-awareness is a key aspect of self-development. Daniel Goleman, in his book *Working With Emotional Intelligence*, highlights self-awareness as being the foundation for outstanding performance at work. Developing self-awareness, and other aspects of emotional competence described by Daniel Goleman, are directly linked to outstanding performance as a manager. For example, a study of top executives at fifteen global companies, including Pepsi, Volvo and IBM, concluded that success at the highest levels could be attributed to emotional intelligence rather than to technical and intellectual competence.

Goleman suggests that self-awareness involves:

- recognizing what emotions you are feeling and why
- being able to accurately assess your strengths and limitations
- having self-confidence.

RECOGNIZING WHAT EMOTIONS YOU ARE FEELING AND WHY

Our emotions and feelings affect the way we behave, i.e. what you say and do. All human relationships are based on our behaviour towards each other. Behaviour can be likened to the visible part of an iceberg – it's just the visible part of what's going on inside your head. Therefore understanding your emotions and feelings, and the effect they have on behaviour, can help you to:

- understand why you behave like you do
- interpret other people's behaviour.

It involves taking time out to 'think'. So much happens each day in the interactions which form human relationships. At the same time, the pace of life means that most people feel far too busy to stop and think about how they relate to people and the effects it has on their relationships. According to Goleman, and an ever increasing number of organizations, it's an investment well spent.

ACTIVITY 2

Consider the following aspects of recognizing your emotions as identified by Goleman. Try to identify at least one example of when you did each one during the last week.

Identify an occasion from the last week when, at work, you:	Your example:
■ Consciously identified what emotions you were feeling and why	
■ Realized the link between your feelings and your behaviour (i.e. something you did or said)	
■ Recognized how your feelings were directly affecting your performance at work	
■ Were aware of how your values and principles affected the way you behaved at work.	

FEEDBACK

Although the activity is very subjective, the ease at which you completed it is likely to be an indication of how attuned you are to your emotions and the effect they have on your behaviour. Becoming more attuned is a life's journey; recognizing the value of becoming more attuned and beginning the journey can start at any time.

ACCURATE SELF-ASSESSMENT

As you would expect, accurate self-assessment involves being aware of your strengths and limitations. But accurate self-assessment is not just about making an inventory at a particular point in time. It's about being constantly open to feedback from your own observations, and others, and using that feedback to develop.

ACTIVITY 3

Below are some of the behaviours people show if they can accurately make self-assessments as identified by Goleman. Can you recognize yourself? Again try to identify an occasion within the last week when you did each one.

Identify an occasion from the last week when, at work, you:	Your example:
■ Consciously identified either a strength or a weakness in yourself ■ Reflected on your behaviour and learned from it – i.e. will do something differently next time ■ Were open to candid feedback from another person.	

FEEDBACK

Being able to accurately identify your strengths and weaknesses is essential if you want to take your self-development along a structured path. But it's not easy. Again it involves making a conscious decision to spend time on an on-going basis thinking about your behaviour. It also involves being open to feedback from others. The ability to receive feedback and, when appropriate, using it is inextricably linked to the next aspect of self-awareness – having self-confidence.

HAVING SELF-CONFIDENCE

Self-confidence is that almost indefinable quality which makes such a significant difference to the way we run our lives. Like some curious 'factor X', you will certainly know those times when you have it, and those times when you don't have it. You will immediately recognize it in others, and from time to time, if you are like most people, you will find yourself wishing you had more of it. But what, exactly, is self-confidence?

When you are self-confident you will feel and behave in certain ways that signal, both to you and to the rest of the world, that you feel good about yourself. When asked to describe that self-confident feeling, a number of senior managers made the following comments:

'When I'm feeling confident I'm prepared to tackle more or less anything that comes up. I know that no matter what happens I'll be able to cope – one way or another.'

'When my confidence is high I look forward to new and challenging situations. It's as though I know that even if something doesn't work out, I won't fall apart. It might be a setback, but it won't be the end of the world.'

'I feel able to start new projects, meet new people, take risks. I don't put things off because I'm worried about failure. I just go for it.'

'I feel good about myself – as though I have value. I feel that what I have to say may not always be right, but that it's as valid and important as anything other people might have to say.'

When those same managers were asked to describe their view of themselves when they were lacking in confidence, their answers were very different:

'When I'm not confident I feel very unsure about my ability to do things – especially new things. Even though I know, at an intellectual level, that I've got the necessary skills and experience I just doubt my own ability … in fact, I feel sure that I'll make a total mess of everything.'

'When my confidence is low I sometimes feel paralysed by indecision. I don't want to take the initiative because I feel sure that I'm going to get it wrong, so it's better to do nothing.'

'When I'm lacking self-confidence I just want to stay with the familiar … projects, people, situations, whatever. I try to avoid anything that might be viewed as confrontational … because at those times I always feel sure that other people will get the better of me.'

'When I don't feel confident I'm very unsure of myself. I tend to keep my views to myself, I find it very hard to say no, and if I come up against someone who is in self-confident mode I always give way.'

The activity below will give you an opportunity to think about the events and people, which affect your confidence.

ACTIVITY 4

Answer the following questions honestly, as they will help you to understand who and what is most likely to impact on your confidence. To preserve confidentiality, you may prefer to write your answers to the questions on a separate sheet of paper.

1   In what circumstances do you feel most confident?

2a Who are the people who make you feel most confident?

2b What do these people say or do to increase your confidence?

3   When do you feel least confident?

4   What is it that causes you to lose confidence? Which situations or people? Which actions or attitudes?

FEEDBACK

For everyone, confidence comes and goes. Feeling confident is the ideal state. It gives us the feeling that we can cope, accept challenges, take risks and deal with life realistically.

We all have periods in our lives when we feel a loss of confidence. Many managers have commented that at times of low confidence they find themselves asking the silent question: 'When will they find out that I can't really do this, and I'm not as good as they think I am?'. When we are lacking in confidence we doubt our abilities and assume (wrongly) that everyone else doubts our abilities too.

Equally we can experience times when we are over-confident. These often happen when you were adamant that you knew best and were totally unwilling to listen to alternative viewpoints and opinions. It often comes across as being brash or arrogant. By refusing help and disregarding advice you may have found yourself launched on a solitary pathway to disaster. Or maybe you were unrealistic about your capabilities, or you accepted more than your fair share of responsibility and then found yourself drowning in a sea of paperwork.

Your answers to the previous activity should have highlighted for you those particular people and circumstances, which either build or destroy your inner sense of purpose, value and competence.

The keys to building and maintaining a steady and constant level of self-confidence are:

- Recognize that **no-one** is confident all the time, even though they may **appear to be**.
- Avoid comparing yourself to other people. They have their strengths, you have yours.
- Acknowledge your own strengths, skills and abilities – use them and build on them.
- Always remember that if you **look** confident and **sound** confident, that's how people will perceive you. (They will have no idea about what's going on inside your head.)
- Learn and constantly practise assertive behaviour – we look at that more closely in Section 2.

Setting personal goals

The second key aspect of ongoing personal development is connected to the process of life planning and personal goals. For most people, having specific (and achievable) personal goals, gives their life meaning and purpose. They have something to aim for and something to look forward to.

Personal goals can be:

- Highly personal, e.g. learn to ride a bicycle, overcome my stutter, lose 4 kilograms in weight.
- Career orientated, e.g. become Corporate Head within 18 months, move onto the Management Spine within two years.

- Work orientated, e.g. create a forum for the team to discuss operational difficulties by January 31.
- Skills orientated, e.g. develop project management skills by April.
- Financial, e.g. save to buy retirement home in Portugal, start a Savings Plan to pay for children to go through university.

Personal goals can be short, medium or long-term (one week, six months, ten years); they can be small or large; easily achievable or requiring considerable effort and even personal sacrifice to achieve. There are no right or wrong personal goals – each person sets their own targets according to their preferences, desires and needs.

The keys to setting and achieving personal goals include:

1   Make sure that your goal, target, objective or outcome (these words are all interchangeable and mean the same thing) is SMART:
    S   Specific – are clear and unambiguous
    M   Measurable – you'll know when it has been achieved
    A   Achievable – you've got the capabilities and resources to achieve it
    R   Relevant – it really matters to you!
    T   Time related – always set a target date for achieving a goal.

2   Break each large goal into a series of smaller, achievable steps. For example, purchase a retirement home in Spain in 2010 may include the following steps:
    Step 1: Investigate Spanish properties (2004)
    Step 2: Sell boat to raise capital for deposit (2006)
    Step 3: Purchase property – irrespective of condition if price and location are right (2007)
    Step 4: Sell existing UK home and move to a smaller property – reduced mortgage payments will support second mortgage in Spain (2007)
    Step 5: Spend annual holidays in property preparing property for retirement (2007–2010).

Any plan can always be amended in the light of new information or even changes to what you want. However, by making any sort of plan you are taking over control of where you want to get to rather than leaving things to take a course, which may or may not be what you want.

'If you don't know where you are going, how will you know when you get there?'

Alice in Wonderland, Lewis Carroll

ACTIVITY 5

Think about your goals for the future. Where do you want to get to and how do you want to get there? Your goals could be related to highly personal achievements, finance, career, home or family or anything else you choose.

1   Make a note of your goals.

2   For each goal you identify, note down the small steps you need to take which, when put together will lead you towards the achievement of your goal.

FEEDBACK

Your response will form the basis of an on-going personal development plan. What's important is that you have a plan which you use as a working document and review, update and amend it accordingly.

Acquiring new skills and knowledge

The third key aspect of personal development is taking the opportunity to develop your skills as a manager and the 'technical' competencies related to your job. As shown in Figure 1.1, it should be a continual cycle of learning with you proactively searching out opportunities.

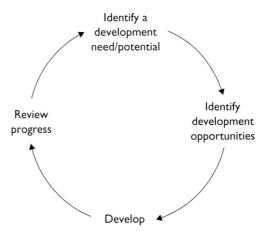

Figure 1.1   Development cycle

Developing is often seen as being synonymous with training courses. However, this is not the only, or necessarily the best way, in which learning can take place. You can also:

- **Learn from other people's experience.** Observing and talking to other people is a particular rich and usually readily available way to learn.
- **Read.** References in this workbook provide a useful starting point. Take out what's useful to you and relevant to your workplace.
- **Use web sites.** Again web sites in this Workbook provide a useful starting point – there is a huge amount of information out there. You need to be aware of its potential and use it to select what's useful to you.
- **Undertake development tasks.** Take on a new responsibility with the aim of developing specific skills.
- **Seek feedback** from other people on what you do and how you do it.

What's important is that you use the experiences to learn and develop yourself so that you move forward as a person both inside and outside work.

EFFECTIVE LEARNING

You can read, watch a video, attend a training course, and learn nothing. In fact, we're bombarded with information and experiences almost continually; most of which we forget because we just passively receive it.

One model which explains how we learn most effectively was developed by an American researcher D.A. Kolb. Kolb's model identifies four processes involved in effective learning as shown in Figure 1.2.

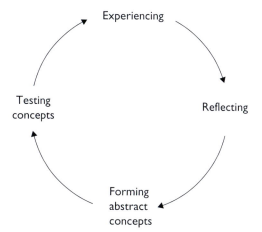

Figure 1.2 Kolb's learning cycle

Kolb argues that effective learning involves:

- **Experiencing** (i.e. doing something).
- **Reflecting, or thinking out, what happened.** In addition to an 'experience', many things, such as reading or observing other people, can feed into the 'reflecting' stage. What's important is that you process information in order to learn from it.
- **Forming abstract concepts.** This is the ideas stage. It involves drawing conclusions from the 'reflections' and forming ideas as to how they can be applied.
- **Testing concepts.** In this stage you test out the ideas. If it gives a successful outcome you will use what you have learned when you do it next time (i.e. back to the 'experiencing' stage). If not then you go round to reflection … and so the cycle continues.

ACTIVITY 6

In which areas do you think you will develop your skills and knowledge over the next 12–18 months?

Divide your list into:

- Work-related skills

- Non-work-related skills

When considering your management skills, try to pinpoint specific areas in which you would like to improve your management skills.

FEEDBACK

To keep up the momentum of developing yourself, you need to be proactive and constantly ask yourself the questions:

- What do I want to do?

- What skills and knowledge do I need to develop to do it?

You may have already identified work-related skills through your organization's performance appraisal system. Working at its best, performance appraisal with your line manager should help you identify skills and knowledge you currently need and those that you want to develop for the future.

Learning summary

1 Personal development is about:

- developing greater self-awareness
- setting personal goals
- acquiring new skills and knowledge.

2 Developing greater self-awareness involves:

- recognizing what emotions you are feeling and why
- being able to accurately assess your strengths and limitations
- having self-confidence.

3 The keys to building self-confidence are:

- recognize that no-one is self-confident all of the time (even though they may appear to be)
- avoid comparing your skills and competences with other people's
- acknowledge your own skills, strengths and abilities
- learn and constantly practise assertive behaviour
- if you look and sound confident, others will believe that you are confident.

4 Personal goals give development a sense of direction and purpose. They need to be SMART:

   ■ **S**pecific
   ■ **M**easurable
   ■ **A**chievable
   ■ **R**elevant
   ■ **T**ime related.

5 Acquiring new skills and knowledge involves being proactive in searching out development opportunities.

Reference

Goleman, Daniel (1997) *Working with Emotional Intelligence*, Bloomsbury Publishing plc

Section 2   The confident manager

Introduction

Confident people use assertive behaviour. Therefore being assertive is a key management skill. It's about stating your opinions honestly and directly. It's also about being able to ask for what you want, saying what you don't want and having the courage to say 'No' when 'No' feels right and appropriate.

Many people are unclear about assertiveness and often confuse being 'assertive' with being 'aggressive'. In this section of the workbook we shall be looking at ways in which you can develop your ability to be assertive, regardless of the situation in which you find yourself, or the people with whom you have to deal.

What's your style?

Every moment of every day, at home and at work, you choose the way you respond to people and situations. In most situations, your response will be either:

- aggressive
- non-assertive (sometimes referred to as passive), or
- assertive.

You may find yourself choosing to operate within one of these modes of behaviour most of the time, or you may find yourself responding aggressively sometimes, with some people; non-assertively sometimes, with some people, and assertively at other times, with other people. You may be perfectly happy with this state of affairs, or you may, like most people, wish that you could be more in control of your feelings and your responses. If this is the case, the first step to changing the way you behave is to understand the differences between these three modes of behaviour.

ACTIVITY 7

What do you think are the differences between aggressive, non-assertive and assertive behaviour? For each of the headings below, give three examples of behaviour.

Aggressive behaviour:

1
2
3

Non-assertive behaviour:

1
2
3

Assertive behaviour:

1
2
3

FEEDBACK

AGGRESSIVE BEHAVIOUR

Examples of *aggressive* behaviour include:

- putting your own needs first, every time
- getting your own way, no matter what you have to do to achieve your objective
- making it very difficult for other people to hold a different opinion
- refusing to listen because you **know** you are **right**
- using verbal or physical intimidation such as shouting, swearing, staring, throwing papers around, slamming doors
- taking advantage of people who are behaving non-assertively
- manipulating people who get your own way.

Tony, a senior manager in a teaching hospital, explains his use of aggressive behaviour:

I'm someone who likes to get things done – if there's a decision to be made, let's make it and move on … and I used to get really impatient with people who like to think things through and work more slowly. At meetings I'd push and push and eventually force the team to agree with me. I felt that I was right, and it seemed just a waste of time to spend three hours considering all the possible options and discussing all the 'maybes' and 'what ifs'. I really didn't feel I was being aggressive, I just thought I was being an efficient and effective manager ... until it all blew up in my face! I pushed something through and it went very, very wrong. The team took great delight in describing, in excruciating detail, how I had been in the driving seat – refusing to listen, refusing to discuss the options. I had to agree ... and then look at how I could change my approach. It isn't easy – because I still want to push on when things slow down, but I have to admit that there's been a significant improvement in the way the team performs.

NON-ASSERTIVE BEHAVIOUR

Examples of *non-assertive* behaviour include:

- deliberately avoiding disagreements
- backing down when faced with aggressive behaviour
- putting up with situations which annoy or frustrate you when you could, in fact, do something about it
- saying 'yes' when you really want to say 'no'
- not being honest about how you feel, and not asking for what you want in case others get angry or upset, or think badly of you
- ignoring your own needs and wishes
- always putting other people first
- putting yourself down, either by making jokes about your ability or by making unnecessary apologies.

David, MD of a precision engineering company, explains his use of non-assertive behaviour:

My background is non-technical and non-scientific. I understand trends and marketing and I can spot a good business opportunity; those are my strengths. Because of the nature of the business we have a number of very highly qualified people working here ... I call them The Boffins. They're very bright, very good at what they do ... and I always feel disadvantaged because they know more about the technical side of things than I do. I find myself agreeing with people when I really want to say 'No! That's not what I want.' Instead, I say 'Yes' – because I feel they know more than I do – and then find myself burning with frustration because I've done it again!

ASSERTIVE BEHAVIOUR

Examples of *assertive* behaviour include:

- communicating your needs, wishes, feelings and opinions calmly, clearly, directly, honestly and factually
- recognizing that **everyone** (this means you **and** the rest of the world too) has the right to hold their own views and opinions
- recognizing that other people may operate in a different way to you, and allowing them to work in their own way, at their own pace

- listening carefully to other people, even when you disagree
- saying 'no' when you choose to
- wanting to reach a workable solution and accepting that this may involve a compromise
- choosing to behave non-assertively when this is the most appropriate action to take.

Carole, Operations Director in the leisure industry, describes her experience of using assertive behaviour:

I used to see-saw between being non-assertive and aggressive. I had great difficulty expressing my views and feelings because I felt it was important to keep things 'nice' and 'calm' in the team. I didn't want confrontations or disagreements and I suppose I also felt, as a woman manager, that if I opposed the majority view, then I could be perceived as difficult or argumentative. So I would go along with things and inwardly become more and more angry and upset. And then I'd blow! I'd really lose my temper over some minor problem, and all the frustration I'd been holding in would spill out … it wasn't very pleasant and it certainly wasn't professional. Now that I've learned what being assertive means I feel able to calmly put my point of view and negotiate for a compromise which suits everyone. And, because I know I have those skills, I can afford to be non-assertive when the situation calls for it. For example, I recently went to a meeting with a new and very important client. He behaved abominably to everyone – he was rude and aggressive and totally unreasonable. In the past I would have taken it … and then felt really bad about the situation afterwards. On this occasion I weighed up the situation, decided that walking away with a signed contract was my key objective and number one priority … and so I kept quiet and smiled a lot. That was OK because I achieved my goal … and I felt absolutely fine because I had made a conscious choice to behave the way I did. I think, at subsequent meetings, this person was more than a little surprised at the change in my style, to say the least!

Use the next activity as an opportunity to think about your responses to a variety of different work situations.

ACTIVITY 8

Consider the questions below and then tick the box which most clearly describes the frequency with which you display this behaviour.

		Always	Often	Now and Then	Never
1	I have difficulty dealing calmly with angry people	❏	❏	❏	❏
2	I find myself becoming quite angry if I feel that people are trying to take advantage of me – and I let them know	❏	❏	❏	❏
3	When my views or actions are challenged I feel intimidated	❏	❏	❏	❏

4 Because it is important to me that people hold a good opinion of me I tend to go along with the majority view ❏ ❏ ❏ ❏

5 I prefer a peaceful life, and don't like to make waves ❏ ❏ ❏ ❏

6 In difficult situations I am able to control my emotions and hold my ground ❏ ❏ ❏ ❏

7 I like to be in control of what's happening ❏ ❏ ❏ ❏

8 There are some people who have the knack of making me feel inadequate – and I find myself agreeing with them when I would really prefer not to ❏ ❏ ❏ ❏

9 I can be volatile and quick-tempered when things aren't going my way ❏ ❏ ❏ ❏

10 I make a real effort to seek a win/win outcome ❏ ❏ ❏ ❏

11 I consider that what I have to say is equally as important as anything anyone else might have to say ❏ ❏ ❏ ❏

12 I can say no to colleagues and subordinates, but I find it hard to say no to someone who has power over me ❏ ❏ ❏ ❏

13 I have the confidence to ask for what I want – even if I might risk upsetting someone else ❏ ❏ ❏ ❏

14 In business, the end justifies the means, and I do whatever I think is necessary ❏ ❏ ❏ ❏

15 I think good teamwork depends on a harmonious working atmosphere – so I go out of my way to avoid disagreeing with colleagues ❏ ❏ ❏ ❏

16 I can bite the bullet and say what I think, honestly and directly ❏ ❏ ❏ ❏

17 When problems occur, I automatically assume responsibility for causing the problem ❏ ❏ ❏ ❏

FEEDBACK

- If you responded with **always** or **often** to questions 1, 2, 7, 9, 14, then you are likely to be adopting a fairly aggressive attitude in your working relationships.
- If you responded with **always** or **often** to questions 3, 4, 5, 8, 12, 15, 17, then you are likely to be responding to work situations with a fairly non-assertive attitude.
- If you responded with **always** or **often** to questions 6, 10, 11, 13, 16, then you are likely to be responding to work situations with assertive behaviour and communication.

Whichever type of behaviour you normally adopt, whether aggressive, non-assertive or assertive, your style has consequences for you, your work colleagues and the people with whom you share your life.

ACTIVITY 9

For each mode of behaviour – aggressive, non-assertive and assertive – consider the ways in which this approach might impact on you, your colleagues and work situations.

Aggressive behaviour

(a) List two consequences which your aggressive behaviour might have for you personally:
1
2

(b) List two consequences which your aggressive behaviour might have upon your colleagues:
1
2

(c) List two consequences which your aggressive behaviour might have upon work situations:
1
2

Non-assertive behaviour

(a) List two consequences which your non-assertive behaviour might have for you personally:
1
2

(b) List two consequences which your non-assertive behaviour might have upon your colleagues:

1

2

(c) List two consequences which your non-assertive behaviour might have upon work situations:

1

2

Assertive behaviour

(a) List two consequences which your assertive behaviour might have for you personally:

1

2

(b) List two consequences which your assertive behaviour might have upon your colleagues:

1

2

(c) List two consequences which your assertive behaviour might have upon work situations:

1

2

FEEDBACK

THE CONSEQUENCES OF YOUR AGGRESSIVE BEHAVIOUR

These can be long-term and potentially quite serious, both for you and everyone around you. They include:

- health problems such as ulcers, hypertension, migraine, exhaustion
- feelings of guilt or regret
- breakdown of communication
- loss of trust and respect
- isolation from colleagues and friends
- short-term and long-term damage to projects resulting from:
  - shortage of information: people are unwilling to confront you with the truth because they know how you are most likely to react
  - shortage of specialist knowledge: you haven't given people a genuine opportunity to contribute

- limited access to the grapevine
- inability to call in 'favours': you don't help anyone, so why should they help you?
■ short-term and long-term damage to career prospects.

If you regularly use aggressive behaviour, you may reap short-term rewards, such as getting your own way or achieving power over others. The down side is that people will seek to avoid you and, wherever possible, they will make sure that you are excluded from developmental projects which require a creative and organic approach. Ultimately, people will work against you.

THE CONSEQUENCES OF YOUR NON-ASSERTIVE BEHAVIOUR

These can be equally serious, and include:

■ health problems, such as depression, lower back pain, digestive problems, insomnia
■ feelings of anger, frustration and self-pity
■ a downward spiral of low confidence and low self-esteem
■ loss of respect
■ breakdown of work relationships as people realize that they are able to take advantage of you ... and then they feel guilty
■ short-term and long-term damage to projects resulting from:
  - missed deadlines: your inability to say no means that you (and your team) take on unrealistic amounts of work and then are unable to complete on time
  - soaring costs: if you aren't able to deal with aggressive colleagues, spending can quickly get out of control, or you can find yourself burdened with many 'nice' but expensive and unnecessary resources
  - poor teamwork: your inability to take a firm line with aggressive colleagues may lead to squabbles, arguments, confrontations and, ultimately, a total breakdown of working relationships on the team
  - ill-conceived ideas: because you find yourself unable to control aggressive colleagues you could find yourself held responsible for an outbreak of expensive mistakes resulting from people realizing they can be as outrageous and experimental as they like
■ short-term and long-term damage to career prospects.

If you regularly use non-assertive behaviour you may often reap short-term rewards, such as avoiding unpleasantness or keeping everyone happy. The down side is that you will become increasingly frustrated and anxious as people begin to assume that you will agree to their demands. You will feel that you are losing control and that your preferences, opinions and ideas carry little weight with the team.

THE REWARDS OF ASSERTIVE BEHAVIOUR

The benefits include:

■ fewer stress-related health problems
■ improved self-confidence, self-esteem and self-respect
■ increased respect from others

- improved work relationships as people begin to:
  - gain confidence in your honesty and openness
  - realize that you say what you mean, and mean what you say
  - recognize that you are a 'safe pair of hands'
  - know where they stand
  - feel free to make suggestions and offer up creative ideas
  - willingly share information
- short-term and long-term benefits for projects include:
  - consistent achievement of objectives: because all your agreements are realistic, deadlines are met and spending remains within budget
  - improved teamwork: the aggressive people realize that they will not be able to intimidate you, the non-assertive people recognize they will be listened to. Everyone begins to understand that you are prepared to discuss, negotiate and – where necessary – compromise
- short-term and long-term career benefits.

People begin to realize that you have the confidence to voice your opinions and ideas reasonably and calmly. They come to see you as someone who will not be intimidated or manipulated; who will work at creating harmonious relationships and who operates with a high degree of firmness, integrity and honesty.

Assertive behaviour in action

Being assertive involves operating from a position where you recognize that:

- you have the right to be heard **and so does everyone else**
- you have the right to hold your own views, opinions and beliefs **and so does everyone else**
- you have something to contribute **and so does everyone else**
- you have the right to disagree and to say 'no' **and so does everyone else**.

The aggressive position is, generally, '**I alone have these rights**', whilst the non-assertive position is '**Everyone has these rights ... except me**'.

ASSERTIVE COMMUNICATION

Assertive communication consists of three simple steps:

> **1** Listen and acknowledge that you have heard the other person's point of view. Ask open questions if you need more information.
> **2** Express clearly and calmly your own position and feelings.
> **3** Make constructive suggestions about what could or should be next.

Step 1 Demonstrate that you've heard and understood

The first step in the process involves making a clear and simple statement which acknowledges whatever has been said. This is important because, if you are dealing with an aggressive person who feels that what they have said has been ignored or brushed aside, then they will become even more aggressive. Non-assertive people will have great difficulty in repeating their question or request, but will inwardly burn with anger and frustration. This can prove to be an explosive combination which may ignite sometime in the future, when you are least expecting it.

Step 2 Express your own feelings and views. Find out more, if you need to

Be direct and honest, and don't be frightened to use 'I' and 'my' statements like:

- 'I'd like it if …'
- 'I'd prefer it if …'
- 'I think that …'
- 'I feel …'
- 'In my opinion …'
- 'My view is that …'

Don't jump to conclusions, and be prepared to take the time to find out more. Ask open how? why? what? when? and where? questions like:

- How do you think we should deal with this?
- What, in your view, is the main problem?
- What changes would you like to see?
- What would your approach be?

Even if someone's opinions are diametrically opposed to yours, do remember that they have the right to hold their own opinions. But also remember that being assertive is about maintaining your own position, even when someone is being aggressive and pushing you hard.

Step 3 Make constructive suggestions as to what might happen next

Often it's not enough just to say 'No' or 'That's not what I want'. Be prepared to make suggestions or offer alternatives. For example:

- 'My view is that we have to proceed very carefully with this, but we could think about …'
- 'I feel that right now would be the wrong time to launch a new campaign. Even so, I recognize your concern, and it would be helpful to know if you think there is another time, later this year, when we could introduce these new ideas.'
- 'I'm very concerned that you haven't been able to meet the deadline we agreed. The key step we need to take now is to create a plan to make sure that the job is finished by the weekend. What do you suggest?'

ACTIVITY 10

For the purpose of this activity, imagine that a colleague has said to you:

'I've been thinking about your proposal for upgrading our customer response times and, to be honest, I just don't think it's going to work. I've come up with a different system and I'm going to put it to the board tomorrow … you don't mind, do you?'

1 How might you respond **aggressively?**

2 How might you respond **non-assertively?**

3 How might you respond **assertively?**

FEEDBACK

'I've been thinking about your proposal for upgrading our customer response times and, to be honest, I just don't think it's going to work. I've come up with a different system and I'm going to put it to the board tomorrow … you don't mind, do you?'

This is a fairly aggressive approach, and an aggressive response might well be something like:

'Oh, so you don't think it's going to work! Well, let me tell you that I've spent a lot of time and effort on these proposals and neither you nor anyone else is going to spoil my presentation tomorrow. So, in a nutshell, yes, I do mind – very much. So don't even think about attempting to hijack my work.'

A person using a non-assertive approach would probably say something like:

- 'Oh … well, I suppose there'll be enough time …'

or even

- 'I'm sorry you think my proposals are so dreadful – perhaps you ought to make the presentation instead of me.'

Someone using assertive communication might say:

- 'The board is expecting me to make my presentation at 3.15 and I expect to talk about my proposals for at least forty-five minutes. As the meeting is due to end at four o'clock there just won't be time for you to make your points. I think it would be better if you could talk to Tom and set up another meeting when you'll have sufficient time to explain your plans in detail.'

Core statements

Working out your core statement can be a very useful exercise when you know, in advance, that you have to:

- confront someone and explain your dissatisfaction
- stand firm to your point of view in the face of strong opposition
- ask for something you want
- refuse a request.

To create a core statement, simply focus on your objective. Think about what you want to achieve as a result of the communication. Here are some examples of core statements which match the list given above.

CONFRONT SOMEONE AND EXPLAIN YOUR DISSATISFACTION

- 'I'm extremely concerned by your sales figures to date and I need to see an improvement by the end of the month.'
- 'I feel that the way you answered questions at that meeting was inappropriate and unacceptable because you used out-of-date statistics. I would like you to update your information and then arrange another meeting so we can go through the data again.'
- 'I've noticed that your team is not producing the results that we agreed would be a minimum acceptable level of performance. I'd like you to prepare a report, by Wednesday, outlining the steps you will take to improve performance.'

STAND FIRM TO YOUR POINT OF VIEW IN THE FACE OF STRONG OPPOSITION

- 'I understand your concerns, but I am convinced, having seen the lab report, that we have no alternative but to abandon the project.'
- 'I can see this is important to you, but, in my opinion, the plan won't work because there isn't enough in the budget to cover all the additional costs.'
- 'I can see why you think we ought to wait, but, in my opinion, if we're going to do this, we need to do it now before we lose our competitive edge.'

ASK FOR SOMETHING YOU WANT

- 'I recognize that money is tight, but I really need another member of staff if we're to reach the targets we've agreed.'
- 'I know there have been difficulties in the past, but I really need to spend some time in the Amsterdam plant, if I'm going to find a solution to the problem.'
- 'I can see why you don't want another delay, but, in my opinion, further tests are absolutely necessary because I need to make sure that the network will support the software.'

Your core statement should be your bottom line, ideal outcome. Of course, as part of the process of searching for a win/win outcome you may have to negotiate and, to some extent, compromise. But, at the very least, if you give your core statement some serious thought **before** the encounter, you will have a clear idea of what you want the outcome to be.

Use the next activity as an opportunity to create a core statement which you can use in a work-related situation.

ACTIVITY 11

Think about a current work-related situation in which you need to use an assertive approach. Take the opportunity to tackle the situation assertively and then address the following points.

1   Provide a brief description of the situation.

2   What is your core statement? (This should reflect your ideal outcome.)

3   How many times did you use your core statement?

4   What was the final outcome, and how does this compare to your core statement?

Saying 'no!'

Many people have great difficulty with refusing requests and saying 'No!' An aggressive refusal to a reasonable request can cause terrific resentment: 'I only asked if I could move my office and she went ballistic!' A non-assertive refusal can leave the questioner wondering whether the answer was yes or no: 'I went in, asked if I could change the schedules, he rambled on for nearly twenty minutes and I've come out of his office and I still don't know. What a waste of time!'

ACTIVITY 12

List four reasons why people might feel reluctant to say 'No!'

1

2

3

4

FEEDBACK

People often mistakenly believe that if they say no, people will:

- get angry and cause a scene
- feel resentful and, at a later date, take some kind of revenge
- spread gossip and rumour about the refusal
- perceive the person saying 'no' in a very negative way.

Robin, a Process Engineer, explains:

I just hate having to say No. I always feel guilty, and I always think that people will feel angry or let down if I refuse a request. So I can never really win. If I say No, I feel guilty or anxious … and I always seem to spend ages apologizing. If I say Yes, I often feel irritated or frustrated because, afterwards, I wish I'd had the courage to say No. It's hopeless.'

If you are caught in a similar spiral, the key points to remember are:

- When you say 'No', you are merely refusing the request and not rejecting the person
- Refusals can be simple, open and honest statements.

NO, WITH A REASON

If you feel it is appropriate, you can soften your refusal by giving a reason for saying 'no':

- 'No, I can't approve an increase to your budget *because* I'm waiting for the results of the internal audit'
- 'No, I can't extend the deadline *because* the client has to ship the delivery on Thursday'.

NO, WITH AN ALTERNATIVE

Offering an alternative is another technique you can use when you feel that a straightforward 'no' might be inappropriate, for example when dealing with an important client or a very senior colleague.

'No, I can't promise that I'll be able to meet your deadline. I can, however, assure you that I can complete the project by the 22nd'

'No, I don't feel that that approach would get the results we need. What I would like to suggest is that we talk to the legal department before we make a decision'.

SIMPLE NO

Sometimes a simple, straightforward 'no' is all that is required. Don't apologize and don't beat around the bush. Just calmly and clearly say 'No'.

- ■ 'No, I'm not prepared to authorize that expenditure'
- ■ 'No, I'm not willing to agree to that'.

BROKEN RECORD NO

The broken record is a useful technique when you find yourself dealing with manipulative or aggressive people who will simply not take 'no' for an answer. In some situations you will find it useful to work out what your core statement is before you get involved in the conversation.

You: **No, I can't promise that I'll be able to meet your deadline**. I can, however, assure you that **I can complete the project by the 22nd**.

Client: But you've never let me down before!

You: And I don't intend to let you down this time. **I can't promise that I can meet your deadline** because the specification has been changed and it's now very complex. I can promise that **I can complete the project by the 22nd**.

Client: But surely, if you pull out all the stops, get extra people in …

You: Because the specification has been changed the nature of the project has changed. If we had stayed with the original ideas I could have completed in time to meet your deadline. But now **I can't promise to do that. I can finish and deliver by the 22nd**.

Client: But the contract states that the project will be done by the 9th.

You: Yes, you're right. But the contract describes the original specification. The new specification requires a great deal more work, and **I can't promise to finish by the 9th, which was the original deadline. I can assure you that I can deliver everything, to your new specification, by the 22nd**.

The key points to remember, when using the broken record technique, are to keep your nerve and continue to repeat your core statement.

Your rights

As we have already mentioned, everyone (that means you **and** the rest of the world) has certain rights. These are shown in Figure 2.1, and you may find it helpful, as part of your assertiveness strategy, to photocopy the list and keep it beside your desk as a constant reminder.

You have the right to:

- ■ **Say No**
- ■ **Express your views, opinions and beliefs** (even if they are different from the mainstream)
- ■ **Ask for what you want** (while recognizing that you might not always get it)
- ■ **Change your mind** (in light of new information or circumstances)
- ■ **Make mistakes** (because everyone does)
- ■ **Not know or understand** (because you can't be expected to know and understand everything)
- ■ **Make your own choices** (because you know what you need and what suits you best)
- ■ **Be yourself**

Figure 2.1   A part of assertiveness is knowing your rights

Assertive body language

When practising assertiveness, you need to make sure that your attitude, words and non-verbal communication all match. Body language is a powerful form of communication. If, for instance, you say something like 'I'm not prepared to support you on this one', while at the same time smiling a sickly smile and wringing your hands, then your listener will know that he has got you in a tight corner.

ACTIVITY 13

List three examples of assertive **non-verbal** communication:

1

2

3

FEEDBACK

There are a number of body language signals you can give to show that you are prepared to listen, but you really do mean what you say. These include:

- standing or sitting upright and straight
- not fidgeting. By keeping your movements to a minimum you will give an impression of calmness and authority
- looking the other person squarely in the eye without staring. Staring is aggressive, and being unable to make eye contact is often perceived as non-assertive, or even shifty
- matching the expression on your face to the words you are using. A stony, impassive face can be aggressive, and a hesitant or fixed smile can be perceived as inappropriate and non-assertive
- maintaining an even, well-modulated tone of voice. Shouting, or speaking very softly and very slowly through clenched teeth are aggressive techniques. Non-assertive people often speak hesitantly and allow their words to trail away at the end of sentences.

The next activity will give you an opportunity to record your progress as an assertive manager.

ACTIVITY 14

This activity is designed to help you to keep a journal of work-related events and situations where you need to use assertiveness skills. You may decide to complete the activity in this workbook, or you may prefer to photocopy the sheet and, for the sake of confidentiality, keep it in a separate folder.

Situation Give a brief description of the situation, together with your reasons for choosing to use assertiveness skills. Include a note of your core statement.

Encounters Briefly describe your encounters with other people involved in the situation. Include a note of their approach (aggressive, non-assertive, assertive) and your responses.

Outcome Briefly describe the outcome of the situation and the way in which this compares with your core statement.

Learning points Note down the learning points you have gained from this situation. What went well? What was difficult? What will you repeat in the future, and what will you avoid? If you had the opportunity to re-run the same situation all over again, what might you do differently?

Learning summary

1   Aggressive behaviour is demonstrated by:
   - putting your own needs first and doing whatever it takes to get your own way
   - making it impossible for other people to hold a different opinion
   - using verbal or physical intimidation – shouting, swearing and so on
2   Non-assertive behaviour is demonstrated by:
   - putting up with annoying and frustrating situations because you don't want to 'make waves'
   - saying yes, when you really want to say no

- ignoring your own needs and wishes and always putting other people first
- going out of your way to avoid disagreements

3 Assertive behaviour, which stems from self-confidence, is demonstrated by:

- communicating your wishes, opinions and feelings openly, honestly and directly. Saying what you mean, and meaning what you say
- recognizing that you have rights, and everyone else has those rights too
- saying 'No' when you choose to
- wanting to reach a workable solution and a win/win outcome

4 Assertive communication involves:

- **Step 1**: Listening and discussing. Asking questions to make sure you understand
- **Step 2**: Expressing, calmly and clearly, your own views and opinions. Using 'I' and 'my' statements
- **Step 3**: Making constructive suggestions about what could happen next

5 A core statement is a brief description of the outcome you hope to achieve when you need to:

- confront someone
- maintain your position or point of view
- ask for something
- say no

6 Techniques for saying 'No':

- No with a reason
- No with an alternative
- Simple No
- Broken record No

7 Assertive body language involves:

- good posture – standing or sitting upright and straight
- not fidgeting
- maintaining steady eye contact
- matching the expression on your face to the words you are using
- Maintaining an even, well-modulated tone of voice.

Section 3   The stress manager

Introduction

Everyone gets stressed from time to time. You won't ever totally eradicate stress from your life because stress is usually caused by external situations. So, unless you choose to live alone, on a desert island, with all your needs continuously provided for, there will always be stressful people and situations in your life.

The key to success is learning how to cope with stress. In this section we will be focusing on the factors, which create stress, and the tools and techniques you can use to improve and manage your response to those factors.

Pressure or stress?

Some people thrive on pressure. They actually **need** pressure to help them make that extra effort to achieve their objectives and to help them feel they are living, rather than just existing. Keith, a partner in a management consultancy, explains:

I enjoy feeling that time is rushing past and I'm chasing after it. I need to be under pressure. When things slow down and get easy, I have to create new situations – challenges, hurdles, whatever you want to call them – otherwise I feel that life is just passing me by. I'm not a laid-back person … I get bored easily and I need constant mental stimulation. I do my best work under pressure … show me an impossible deadline, and I'll show you a happy man.

Some element of pressure is necessary for everyone. People who have little or no pressure in their lives – those with few interests and who are unable to take part in an active social life – are prone to many of the illnesses which affect people with too much pressure. Although the medical profession and stress management experts agree that some pressure is desirable, the problems arise when the pressure develops into stress.

ACTIVITY 15

1 How do you feel when you are working under pressure? List four symptoms (mental, emotional or physical) which indicate to you that you are under pressure.

   1
   2
   3
   4

2 How do you feel when you are stressed? List four symptoms (mental, emotional or physical) which indicate to you that you are stressed-out.

   1
   2
   3
   4

FEEDBACK

THE SYMPTOMS OF PRESSURE AND THE SYMPTOMS OF STRESS

You may have identified some of the following as the symptoms of pressure and stress feeling:

Symptoms of pressure	Symptoms of stress
■ challenged	■ drained
■ excited	■ bored
■ energized	■ exhausted
■ stretched	■ indecisive
■ confident	■ uncertain
■ creative	■ anxious or depressed
■ competent	■ incompetent
■ valued	■ undervalued or neglected
■ powerful	■ powerless
■ moving forward	■ stuck

The excitement of pressure can easily turn into the nightmare of stress, as Anna, a Sales Director, explains:

We were opening up retail outlets all over Europe and I was enjoying every minute of my job – the deadlines, the high-level meetings, the targets – it was great. Then we got some bad press about an environmental issue, and sales started to fall. At that point one of our major suppliers pulled out, and then, on top of everything else my immediate boss, the Sales Director, resigned and I took on his job, together with all his additional responsibilities. The pressure was mounting, and I stopped feeling excited and motivated and started feeling worn-out and quite ill. Then, as if I didn't have enough to cope with, my partner was badly injured in a car accident. Because he works from home as a self-employed consultant I was having to deal with a lot of his work-related issues as well as my own. I was dashing to the hospital, trying to prove myself in a new and even more demanding job, trying to keep his business afloat and trying to do normal, personal things like shopping and paying the household bills. I struggled on for months, not eating, hardly sleeping, getting more and more uptight and irritable and, in the end, I just snapped. I felt totally overwhelmed by it all … instead of the outgoing, decisive, high-profile person my company needed, I became someone who couldn't make a decision and who, to put it bluntly, couldn't lead a team out of a paper bag.

As well as mental and emotional symptoms, there are a number of stress-related physical symptoms which can sometimes (but not always) signal that pressure has turned to stress. These include:

- eating problems (overeating or loss of appetite)
- sleep disorders (insomnia, wanting to sleep much more than usual or waking up much earlier than usual and not being able to get back to sleep)
- raised blood pressure or palpitations
- nausea and/or vomiting or other digestive problems
- back, shoulder or neck pain which, has not been caused by an injury or a pre-existing condition like arthritis
- icy cold hands or profuse perspiration
- frequent and severe headaches.

What causes stress?

The most common causes of stress are:

- loss of a partner, child or close family member
- getting married or committing to a long-term personal partnership
- loss of a long-term personal partnership through separation or divorce
- retirement
- difficulties with family, friends or neighbours
- relocation or even moving house in the same area
- taking on large new financial commitments (mortgages, major loans, etc.)
- not being able to meet existing financial commitments
- job loss (redundancy or any other reason)

- job promotion or new/additional work responsibilities
- outstanding personal achievement
- accident, surgery, major illness in the family
- going on holiday
- Christmas.

In addition, there are quite specific job-related factors which cause high levels of stress.

ACTIVITY 16

List five factors, which cause stress for you at work:

1
2
3
4
5

FEEDBACK

The most common causes of stress at work, for most people, are:

- working environment
- technology
- job role
- relationships
- career development
- change.

WORKING ENVIRONMENT

A major stressor can be working in an environment that does not suit your personality or temperament. Some people need to work in a tidy, uncluttered and fairly peaceful environment; some people need a constant change of scenery and a steady stream of new faces and new people with whom to engage; some people need light and fresh air, and so on. A senior manager explains how his working environment played a major role in contributing to his stress at work:

Geoff, Senior Accounts Manager with a precision engineering company:

I need peace and quiet so that I can think clearly. I used to have my own office, and that was fine. Then the company decided to go open-plan, top down ... which meant everyone. I found myself working in a space surrounded by people, ringing telephones, comings and goings and conversations. Even when people whispered it drove me crazy! I ended up taking work home and doing at home – at night and at the weekends – what I was paid to do during office hours. It was a nightmare. I was going to resign – it was that bad. Then I talked to some colleagues and found out that it was having an effect on them too. We had a meeting with the MD and hammered out a compromise, which involved setting up some sound-proof screens and reorganizing the desks so that the 'quiet' people all work together. It's fine now.

What can you do to make your work environment less stressful?

First of all, you need to give some careful thought to the kind of environment that suits you best. Do you prefer the mutual support and 'busyness' of an open-plan office? Do you dislike the isolated splendour of a room to your-self? Do you need absolute peace and quiet? Does clutter upset you? Once you have identified whether or not your working environment is causing you stress, then you can start to do something about it. Positive action you could take might include:

- organizing additional screening to isolate your desk from the rest of the room
- personally investing in a really comfortable chair, which suits you, if you are not able to requisition one from the company
- asking for a telephone, which has a flashlight facility, so that you can turn off the ringer bell if the noise is driving you to distraction
- redecorating your office if you are working in dismal or dingy surroundings
- investing one weekend of your time in clearing out the clutter and creating a tidy and streamlined work space.

All of these solutions may take some of your personal time or money (if the company is unwilling to meet your requirements). On one level you may feel that this is unacceptable, but if the required changes mean that you will be less stressed, more comfortable and more content at work, then it will be worthwhile.

TECHNOLOGY

Coping with new technology (this might be new plant and machinery or even a fax or laptop computer) with which you feel less than comfortable can be a major source of stress. Neville, a senior partner in a general practice, explains:

We decided, as a Group Practice, to introduce a computer network. This means that all our files are held on computer, and – so the Practice Manager told me – 'we just had to key-in the prescription and hey presto!'. Within days I was changed from a highly effective professional into a shambling wreck … I couldn't type, and I just couldn't get to grips with the computer at all. Even worse, all of my disasters were witnessed by my patients, who were sitting in my surgery while I fumbled around. In the end I booked myself onto an evening course and got some serious help. Now, I would hate to be without it – but at the start it was a very different story.

What can you do to make technology less stressful?

Accept that we live in a technological age and it just won't go away. The key to success is learning as much as you possibly can. Take advantage of every possible training opportunity, network with friends and colleagues, or even book yourself onto a part-time evening course at your local college.

JOB ROLE

'Job role' covers everything from the amount of responsibility your job entails and the level of decision-making you are empowered to undertake, through to the quantity and quality of resources at your command and the skills-mix of the people on your team. Problems in any of these or similar areas can cause major stress. How one problem leads on to another, in a downward spiral of stress, is illustrated in Figure 3.1 below.

Lack of skills on the team →	Unable to delegate →	**STRESS** → ↓	Increase in personal workload →	**STRESS** ↓
↘ Targets and deadlines not achieved ↓	Insufficient resources →	Targets and deadlines not achieved →	**STRESS** →	Targets and deadlines not achieved ↓
STRESS ↓	Too much responsibility ↓	Insufficient authority → ↓	**STRESS** ↓	Lack of support ↓
Loss of credibility →	**STRESS** →	Loss of confidence →	**STRESS** →	Targets and deadlines not achieved ↖

Figure 3.1   How job role factors can cause stress

What can you do to make your job role less stressful?

The first thing to do is to be clear about the boundaries:

- your organization's objectives and priorities
- lines of authority and communication, both above you and below you
- your responsibilities
- the budget and other resources at your command
- your objectives
- your priorities

Then, be prepared to:

- delegate (you don't have to do **everything**)
- where necessary develop the team (this will leave you free to attend to **urgent and important** tasks)

RELATIONSHIPS

Relationships at work have the potential to cause significant stress. The key ways to improve relationships at work are to:

- remember your rights
- respect everyone else's rights
- recognize that you have your own way of working
- respect other people's ways of working
- use assertiveness skills (say what you mean and mean what you say)
- negotiate and compromise (look for the **win/win** situation).

CAREER DEVELOPMENT

Feeling stuck in an undemanding job can be just as stressful as feeling over-whelmed by too much work, too many responsibilities and a wallchart packed with impossible deadlines.

What can you do to make your career development less stressful?

Network, both within your organization and beyond. Let people know that you are prepared to face new challenges. Look for new opportunities and additional responsibilities within your existing company and, if there are none, start looking around for something else.

CHANGE

Just about everyone has some resistance to change. This is because we know we can deal with the familiar – even if it's boring or otherwise unsatisfactory. Change means something new and unfamiliar. 'Will I be able to cope?', 'Will it be worse than it is now?' and 'What'll happen if I don't like it, or I can't do it?' are quite usual responses when change beckons.

What can you do to make change less stressful?

Perhaps the most important and useful thing you can do is to remember that you have already been through many changes in your life, and survived them all. Taking the first step which led you to where you are now probably meant having to deal with some kind of change. You did it then, you can do it again!

The key steps you can take to help you deal with organization change are:

- get as much information as possible about the proposed changes

- decide if you need to implement some kind of influencing strategy. If so, plan your campaign and put it into action

- look for practical ways in which you can overcome any negative aspects you feel you may have identified

- look for the benefits and see how you can maximize them

- focus on the positive aspects, rather than the negative.

ACTIVITY 17

Complete the chart below by identifying the work-related factors which are stressful for you and the strategies you can implement to either reduce or eliminate the stress:

Cause of stress	Specific stress factors	Action I can take to reduce or eliminate this stress factor
Environment		
Technology		
Job role		
Relationships		
Career development		
Change		

How do you manage your stress?

There's no doubt that, from time to time, everyone gets stressed. And it is also true that everyone, regardless of their circumstances, can take some simple steps to manage that stress. Use the next activity as an opportunity to check whether or not you are already taking the necessary key steps which will help to keep stress to acceptable levels.

ACTIVITY 18

Consider the following questions and complete the chart by ticking the appropriate box.

	Most of the time	Some of the time	Never
I share my worries and concerns with someone I trust			
I have friends with whom I can relax and really be myself			
I take time to be by myself every day, just relaxing and winding down			
I express my feelings and don't just bottle them up			
I have at least one interest or hobby outside of work			
I get involved in activities outside of work which help me to relax			
I can see the funny side of life and enjoy a good laugh			
I take part in some kind of activity which is specifically designed to reduce stress			
I feel reasonably optimistic about the future			
I take some exercise at least once each week			
I'm roughly the right weight for my height, age and build			
I relax and switch off from work by choosing TV or radio programmes, books or music which give me pleasure			
I don't exceed the recommended limits for alcohol consumption			

FEEDBACK

In an ideal situation, in a perfect world, you would be able to answer that you do **all** of these things **most of the time**. Realistically, you should be able to say that you do most of these things **most of the time**. If you found yourself saying that you **never** do **most of these things**, then perhaps it's time to start looking at the way in which stress occurs, and some specific stress management techniques.

Fight or flight?

So far in this workbook we have looked at some of the causes of stress and some of the effects. Now it's time to take a closer look at the *connection* between the causes and the effects.

In the distant past, we lived in caves and hunted for food. Life was simple, basic and very, very dangerous. Over time, human beings evolved a very sophisticated physical response system which allowed them to react appropriately in dangerous situations and take flight and run away very, very quickly from dinosaurs and sabre-tooth tigers; or stand and fight. We humans developed the *Fight or Flight* response to help us to react to dangerous, life-threatening situations.

We no longer live in caves nor do we hunt for food, but, even now, we still have the physical response system which automatically clicks into place whenever we feel threatened. The way this works is shown in Figure 3.2 below.

I Danger				
You perceive a threat to your safety or well-being. This could be a wild animal, but is much more likely to be another driver; an irate customer; a hostile colleague; or a meeting with someone who has power over you. ↓				
		2 The automatic physical response kicks in →		
10 Action stations! Adrenalin and a whole host of associated hormones flood the system, and your body is now ready to run very, very fast, or stand and flight ↑			**3 Heart responds** by beating faster to supply blood more quickly →	**4 Blood responds** Blood pressure rises because the heart is beating faster. Blood clotting agents are released into the bloodstream in anticipation of bleeding from wounds ↓
9 Digestive system responds Bladder and bowels empty to leave the body lighter	**8 Skin responds** Blood drains away from the surface in order to minimize bleeding from wounds. Perspiration increases in order to cool the body while running or fighting ←	**7 Brain responds** Blood flow to the brain increases in anticipation of the need for quick thinking ←	**6 Liver responds** by releasing cholesterol to provide energy ←	**5 Lungs respond** Breathing rate is increased to ensure a good supply of oxygen ←

Figure 3.2 The automatic fight or flight response

We become aware of our readiness to deal with danger because we experience the following physical symptoms:

- palpitations
- dizziness
- breathlessness
- cold hands and feet
- perspiration
- vomiting and/or diarrhoea.

We are physically ready to run or fight, but the problem is that, in most cases, we are not in a position to do either. Although we have perceived that we are in some kind of dangerous or threatening situation (and this is often sub-conscious), and our bodies have diligently prepared us to deal with the situation, the reality is usually quite different. Instead, we sit in our cars in a two-mile tail-back and quietly fume. Or we smile through gritted teeth and make assurances that yes, we will bring the project in on time. Or we find ourselves attempting to manage a conflict situation between two warring factions, knowing that we hold the responsibility for finding a win/win outcome.

The end result is that, because of the shots of adreno-cortico-trophic hormone, cortisol, adrenalin and noradrenalin which our body has automatically supplied, we are 'on alert' in a big way. Sometimes we snap, lose our temper, shout and throw things around – then we feel better. Sometimes we bottle it up and pretend we're OK. But if we don't have a technique for clearing these hormones out of our system then, after a while, illness sets in. We can suffer from migraines, ulcers and permanently raised blood pressure. If still nothing is done, the body, tired of being in a constant state of preparedness, can really break down, and strokes, heart attacks and burn-out can be the disastrous result. As Sara Paddison says in her book *The Hidden Power of the Heart*.[1]

Research at London University's Institute of Psychiatry, undertaken over a twenty year period, showed that people who bottled up their emotions under stress were likely to be more prone to cancer. Cigarette smoking or eating foods high in cholesterol by themselves had less effect in causing disease than did negative reactions to stress.

Figure 3.3 shows the four stages of the stress response.

Developing the habit of using stress management techniques

Anything can become a habit. It usually starts as an activity we do once, then repeat, and then incorporate into our daily or weekly routine.

Stage 1	Stage 2	Stage 3	Stage 4
We feel threatened	Body and brain prepare to deal with the threat	If we 'fight' or 'take flight', the body utilizes the fats, sugars, hormones and adrenaline which have been released	Hormones, etc. are released and body and brain return to normal

THE DANGER ZONE

⇩ ⇩

Stage 3	Stage 4
We do not 'fight' or 'take flight'. We suppress our emotions. The body does not utilize the fats, sugars, hormones and adrenalin which have been released	We are in a constant state of readiness for 'fight' or 'flight'. Body and brain continue to pump fats, sugars, hormones and adrenalin. Eventually body and brain become exhausted. This leads to illness and, in time, death.

Figure 3.3

Over time the activity becomes a habit, and we do it without question. For example:

- you take the dog for a walk and go through the park
- you do it again
- every time you walk the dog you go through the park
- you don't really know **why**, but you do it. You don't even question the activity because it has become a habit.

ACTIVITY 19

How do you deal with the stress in your life? What techniques do you use? Have you developed any stress reduction habits?
List three things you regularly do to help you to manage your stress.

1

2

3

FEEDBACK

There are numerous techniques you can use to manage the 'fight or flight' response. Even if you make only one of these techniques a habit, you will be making a positive move towards managing the stress in your life.

THE EXERCISE HABIT

Some people thoroughly enjoy exercise and make it a habit to do something every week which physically helps the body to release the build-up of 'fight or flight' hormones. On the other hand, many people (especially busy managers) resist the idea of exercise. Here are some options to consider:

- *Swimming* – exercises all the muscles and is kind to aching backs
- *Golf* – a good way of networking
- *Joining a gym* – another good way to meet people and improve your social life
- *Cycling* – needn't be too demanding, and is a good way to get out in the fresh air
- *Dancing* – although often considered a social activity, also a good way to exercise
- *Yoga* – gentle exercise for people of all ages.

THE INTERESTS HABIT

It is very easy to become so absorbed in a demanding job that you can find yourself **living to work**, rather than **working to live**. To avoid this trap, you need to get involved in at least one absorbing interest that is not, in any way, work-related. Here are some suggestions:

- Join an evening class to learn something new – perhaps another language, or how to cook Asian food or repair watches.
- Take up a hobby which really interests you but for which you have never before allowed time
  - photography, redesigning the garden, furniture restoration, painting. Or play chess, do crosswords, write a book, learn to play the guitar.
- Join a book club and aim to read at least one book (which is not work-related) each week.
- Get involved in voluntary work as a means of giving something back to the community.
- Form a 'dinner club' or a 'wine club' with friends and check out the best treats on offer in your area.
- Visit the theatre, the opera, the ballet, museums or art galleries.

THE COMMUNICATION HABIT

In her book *He Says, She Says,*[2] Dr Lillian Glass makes the key points:

Men and women talk about different things. Women tend to talk about self-improvement, clothes, other people and relationships, while men tend to talk about sports, business, mechanical things, cars and music.

Talking things through is a good safety valve because it helps you to explore feelings and emotions. So research suggests that if you are a man, it's time to start talking about personal issues and, if you're a woman, keep talking. Sharing information at a personal level, with someone you trust, is an important stress management tool.

THE 'BE GOOD TO YOURSELF' HABIT

Get into the habit of giving yourself a treat at least once a week. Think of it as a reward for work well done. Here are some possibilities:

- *Aromatherapy* massage involves the use of essential oils taken from fruit, leaves, flowers and other organic material. Depending on the oil (or combination of oils) which the therapist chooses, the massage can be energizing, balancing, soothing or relaxing
- *Counselling and psychotherapy* give you the opportunity to explore, through talking, deeply personal issues in a safe, one-to-one environment
- *Homeopathy* is a well-respected branch of alternative medicine which seeks to heal the whole person (mind, body and spirit). Homeopathic medicines (most often prescribed in tablet form) are made from minute amounts of natural, organic substances and can be used to treat physical, mental and emotional problems
- *Reflexology* is a form of foot massage which helps to balance the emotions and encourages the body to begin the process of repairing any physical damage or disturbance.

THE MEDITATION HABIT

Meditation is emerging as a stress management tool which has been rigorously examined by the medical and scientific 'establishments' and pronounced both respectable and highly beneficial. Research[3] has shown that repeated meditation establishes new neural pathways which prevent the accumulation of stress effects, making the technique a natural stress release mechanism.

There are many different forms of meditation. *Transcendental meditation* requires the practitioner (you) to sit quietly and silently repeat a simple word or phrase such as 'Peace' or 'I am peaceful' or 'The bottom line' or whatever else takes your fancy. This works because the repetition stills and calms the mind, but it does take some time to learn how to 'switch off' other thoughts. *Yoga meditation* requires you to focus on observing your breath, and *Guided meditation*, which is perhaps the easiest and most accessible technique, simply involves listening to a *guided meditation journey* on cassette tape. As Lisa Davis says in her book *Journeys Within: A Source Book of Guided Meditations*[4], guided meditations are structured, they have a precise beginning, middle and end, and each meditation is a self-contained experience. Guided meditations require no practice, and the benefits and results are immediate.

Use the next activity as an opportunity to create an action plan for stress management.

ACTIVITY 20

1   Check back to Activity 16 in which you identified the factors which cause stress for you at work. Take a moment to add any additional factors which may be appropriate for you in your current situation.

The factors which are currently causing me stress:

2   Identify at least three things you can do to reduce or eliminate these stress factors.
    1
    2
    3

3   Note down the date on which you plan to start using your chosen tools for stress management, and the date (perhaps three months later) on which you plan to review progress.

Date when I'm going to start taking positive action to manage my stress:

Date when I'm going to review my progress:

4   On or after your chosen review date, note down the progress you have made:

Learning summary

1 People under pressure respond by feeling excited, energized, challenged and as though they are moving forward.

2 People under stress respond by feeling exhausted, depressed, indecisive and stuck.

3 When pressure escalates into stress, the body is overloaded with adrenalin and other associated hormones which are supplied by the nervous system as an *automatic* physiological response to perceived danger.

4 It is necessary to have some way to release these hormones from your system. This can be done by losing your temper (road rage is a good example of this technique!), or by using one or more techniques specifically designed to switch the body from 'All systems go, Alert' status to 'Normal, At rest' status.

5 Some common physical symptoms of stress include:
   - eating problems and sleep disorders
   - raised blood pressure, palpitations or breathlessness
   - ulcers, migraines, frequent headaches, muscular pain and
   - illnesses related to the immune system (e.g. colds, flu, etc.)

6 The factors which are most usually responsible for causing stress at work are:
   - work environment
   - technology
   - job role
   - relationships
   - career development
   - change

7 You can effectively manage the stress in your life by developing one or more of the following habits:
   - exercise habit
   - interests habit
   - communication habit
   - 'be good to yourself' habit
   - meditation habit.

References

1 Paddison, Sara (1995) *The Hidden Power of the Heart*, Planetary Publications.
2 Glass, Dr Lillian (1992) *He Says, She Says*, Piatkus.
3 Gerber, Dr Richard (1988) *Vibrational Medicine*, Bear & Company Publishing, 1988.
4 Davis, Lisa (1995) *Journeys Within: a source book of guided mediations*, Findhorn Press.

Section 4   The time manager

Introduction

Generally, there are two basic approaches to time management. Approach number one involves **hoping that there will be enough time** to do everything. Usually there isn't, and people who adopt this hopeful approach quickly find themselves becoming short of time and very, very stressed.

Approach number two involves **taking control of time**. Those people who tackle time management head-on and take control of the time at their disposal find that they benefit in numerous ways.

The main benefit of taking control of your time is that you will reduce personal anxiety and stress because you will be able to:

- manage your workload (you know what you have to do and you organize your time so that you can do it)
- achieve improved results and make fewer mistakes (you can progress steadily from task to task without panic or confusion)
- see exactly what you are achieving (objectives are reached and noted).

In this section of the workbook we will be looking at the specific practical steps you can take in order to take control of your time and make it work for you.

Do you have enough time?

Your relationship with time will depend, to a large extent, on the organization for which you work. You may:

- battle with time, because there is never enough
- be overwhelmed by time, because there is too much; or
- get along OK with time.

ACTIVITY 21

1 How would you describe the relationship between the amount of work you have to do and the amount of time available in which to do the work?

Tick one box only

(a) Generally, I have time on my hands ❑

(b) Generally, there is never sufficient time to get through everything which needs my attention ❑

(c) Although I can't say I always have enough time, the gap between work and time makes me feel challenged and stretched. It's OK. ❑

2 What do you think is the main reason for your relationship with time being the way that it is?

FEEDBACK

The way in which these relationships work are shown in Figure 4.1.

Amount of work you have to get through	Amount of time you have available	How you feel about this relationship
▫ →	◻	**Bored** Undervalued Not reaching your potential ☹
◻ →	▫	**Panic-stricken** Overworked Stressed Unable to cope ☹
◻ →	◻	**Challenged** Steadily working towards achievable objectives ☺

Figure 4.1 Three kinds of relationships we can have with time and work

Maybe, in response to the previous activity, you were able to say that generally, you feel challenged by the work/time relationship, but are able to work steadily towards your objectives. This means that your workload is under control. You will be under pressure to some extent – but this will be a level of pressure which motivates you and gives you the confidence to continue to work hard towards achieving your objectives.

If you responded by saying that your current work/time relationship leaves you bored and with time on your hands, then you are likely to be feeling as though time is passing you by and that you are not achieving your full potential.

If, like many managers, you feel that there is too much work and just not enough time, then you will be suffering from stress, and it is time to look at ways in which you can manage your time more effectively.

Planning your time

At work you have four kinds of time-slots. By recognizing and planning for these different time-slots you can make the most of the time available to you, and organize your workload more effectively.

FIXED TIME-SLOTS

These are the parts of the day (week or month) where you know you have regular, fixed activities. For example:

- First Monday of the month, 9.30–12 noon: Marketing meeting
- Thursday of every week, 10.00–12.30: Team meeting
- Friday of every week: 9 a.m.–5.30 p.m.: checking figures, correlating statistics and data, preparing draft report for Finance team.

FLEXIBLE TIME-SLOTS

These are the times when you attend to urgent/important tasks as well as routine tasks such as correspondence, phone calls, networking and so on.

PERSONAL TIME-SLOTS

These are blocks of time during which you can work on special projects which will move you closer towards achieving your own **personal work objectives**. Personal time-slots should be blocked out in your diary as 'strictly personal, do-not-disturb' time. Managers who don't recognize the importance of personal time-slots are the people who either don't submit projects and reports on time, or who do this work at home in the evening or at the weekend **because there isn't enough time during the work-ing week**.

UNEXPECTED TIME-SLOTS

These are those unexpected chunks of time which crop up now and then. You can't plan for them, because they are **unexpected**, but you can prepare in advance so that you can make the most of them when they occur.

Figure 4.2 shows how one manager has set up his diary to allow for fixed time, flexible time and personal time.

Monday 4 November	Tuesday 5 November	Wednesday 6 November	Thursday 7 November	Friday 8 November
8	8	8	8	8
9 Team meeting	9 Project of planning	9 Flexible time	9 Health & safety	9
10 Fixed time	10 Fixed time	10	10 Fixed time	10
11	11	11	11 Flexible time	11 Flexible time
12	12 Flexible time	12	12	12
1	1	1	1	1
2 Flexible time	2 Flexible time	2 Flexible time	2 Board meeting	2 Flexible time
3	3	3	3 Fixed time	3
4	4	4	4	4
5	5	5	5	5
6	6	6	6	6

Key

These boxes indicate *fixed* time-slots – e.g. regular meetings, etc. which can be entered into the diary in advance

These boxes indicate *personal* time-slots – e.g. times which can be devoted to your own tasks and objectives (e.g. writing reports, gathering data, planning campaigns, etc.)

These boxes indicate *flexible* time-slots – e.g. times when you will attend to correspondence, take phone calls, network with colleagues and suppliers, attend one-off meetings, etc.

Figure 4.2 Diary for week Monday 4 November to Friday 8 November blocked out according to different types of time-slots

One of the keys to effective time management is planning ahead. Obviously you can't do anything about fixed time meetings, and if the Board wants you in Carlisle every Monday morning, and a major account needs you in London every Tuesday morning, and the team needs you in Edinburgh every Wednesday afternoon, then so be it. But if you plan the time **between** fixed time-slots, then you will immediately find that you can manage your workload more effectively.

Use the next activity as an opportunity to experiment with blocking out specific time-slots so that, between fixed time segments, you can plan ahead to give yourself flexible time and personal time.

ACTIVITY 22

Look back through your work diary for the past month or so, and choose a busy week. In the diary sheet below, mark in your *fixed* time-slots. Then divide the remaining time into *flexible* time and *personal* time. Look for ways in which you can save time by grouping similar activities together in the flexible time-slots, and allocate personal time for your own projects.

Monday	Tuesday	Wednesday	Thursday	Friday
8	8	8	8	8
9	9	9	9	9
10	10	10	10	10
11	11	11	11	11
12	12	12	12	12
1	1	1	1	1
2	2	2	2	2
3	3	3	3	3
4	4	4	4	4
5	5	5	5	5
6	6	6	6	6

FEEDBACK

Naturally, everyone's workload is different, but here are some practical suggestions as to how you can plan your week effectively and use your diary as an important management tool.

FIXED TIME

There isn't a great deal you can do about this. The fixed time-slots are those which, to a large extent, are controlled by other people.

FLEXIBLE TIME

This is the time over which you have a great deal of control. A key technique for managing this kind of time is to 'chunk' similar tasks together. For example, if you specifically dedicate three hours to telephone calls then, during that time, you will make many more calls than if you try to 'slot' them in here and there, during the whole of the week. During your three hours you can work down your list and, if a number is engaged, you just move on to the next call. If people are not available, you can leave a message for them to call you back, and you can move on through your list. Other tasks which can be 'chunked' include:

- mail (reading and writing correspondence)
- reading (reports, proposals, journals, etc.)
- preparing proposals or quotations
- networking with colleagues, suppliers or customers.

PERSONAL TIME

This is the type of time-slot which many managers forget to plan. If you have a specific task or project which is your sole responsibility and cannot be delegated, then you really do need to allocate personal time to this.

Rob, a senior manager in retail, explains:

When I moved into management I read all the right books and decided I would keep an open-door policy. It was great for the team because they would pop along at any time and talk through their worries, concerns and problems. But it was a nightmare for me… every time I settled down to do some of my work there'd be a little tap on the door and my heart would sink.

Within six months I was totally stressed out because I couldn't manage my workload. I was getting into the office before everyone else, staying late and taking work home, just to get some peace. Now I take Monday and Wednesday afternoons as personal time. I shut myself into the office, hold calls, ban visitors and just get on. Obviously, if there's a major, major crisis I'll deal with it … but otherwise, as far as the team are concerned, I'm out of the building.

The key to success is to be absolutely determined about keeping some part of the working week for yourself – your own work objectives, your own top work priorities. Look at it this way – if you weren't in the office, it would have to wait or someone else would have to deal with it.

UNEXPECTED TIME-SLOTS

Because unexpected time is, by its very nature, unexpected, you can't block it out in your diary. You never know when it's going to crop up. But you can prepare for it so that, when you have a block of unexpected time, you can turn your attention to a meaningful and productive task, rather than wondering 'What'll I do first?'. Make a list of the tasks you could usefully do if and when an unexpected time-slot occurs (maybe when a scheduled meeting is cancelled). Use the next activity to create a working list of tasks you can usefully turn your attention to during unexpected time.

ACTIVITY 23

List up to five tasks to which you can give your attention if and when an unexpected time-slot occurs. Clearly, these will not be Urgent and Important tasks, but are the things 'I'd like to get around to when I have the time'.

1

2

3

4

5

The list you created in the previous activity should be regularly updated. As soon as one task is completed and out of the way, add another to the bottom of the list. In this way, if unexpected time is presented to you, it won't be wasted.

Managing your diary

Some key tips for managing your diary:

- Use a pencil, so that when appointments change (as they will) alterations can be made easily and you're not left with pages of messy changes.
- Note down sufficient details, as this will help you to prepare in advance:
  - **2.30 Tom Dawson**, when viewed two weeks later, can cause confusion and even delay if you can't remember the key details
  - **2.30 Tom Dawson, re: Nottingham site – take map and working drawings** is much more helpful and useful.

- Estimate the time you are prepared to spend on each task or meeting and note that down, too. Aim to keep within the time-slots you have allocated for each task or meeting, e.g.:
  - **2.30–4p.m. Tom Dawson, re: Nottingham site – take map and working drawings**

  Setting a time for completion will allow you to make realistic follow-on appointments and will also enable you to get away from people who want to waste your time (these are the people who are not taking control of **their** time).

Planning on a daily basis

Careful planning is the cornerstone of good time management, and a 'To Do' list will be of great help to you when planning ahead. To create a working 'To Do' list you need:

- a master list
- a daily list.

YOUR MASTER LIST

Your master list is a single, continuous list, which is maintained in a notebook. It consists of every single thing you have to do. Throughout each day, every time someone asks you to attend a meeting, find out information, write a report, make a telephone call, whatever – you write down the task on your master list. Every time you think of something which you need to do, write it down on your master list. An example is given in Figure 4.3.

- Ring Joe about sales figs
- See Jean re Marshall Bros
- Arrange doctor's appointment
- Flowers for Louise
- 10 p.m. 10 June – meeting with Michael Saunders and Joan Parker re training programme
- See Sally about chairs

Figure 4.3 Example of a master list

DAILY 'TO DO' LIST

Either at the **end** of each working day, or the **beginning of the next** working day, you need to take five or ten minutes to transfer items on your master list onto your daily 'To Do' list.

Making your master list work for you

Step 1   Sort out your master list. There will be *Immediate* tasks and *Future* tasks.

Step 2   Transfer the Future tasks into your diary:

- 10 p.m. 10 June – meeting with Michael Saunders and Joan Parker re training programme

Step 3   Transfer the Immediate tasks into your 'daily To Do' list:

To do Wed. 4 September
- Ring Joe about sales figs
- See Jean re Marsha all Bros
- Arrange doctor's appointment
- Flowers for Louise
- See Sally about chairs

Step 4   Throughout the day, continue to add to your master list. Tick each task on your daily 'To Do' list as it is completed. At the end of the day, your 'To Do' list might look like this:

To do Wed. 4 September
- Ring Joe about sales figs ✓
- See Jean re Marshall Bros
- Arrange doctor's appointment ✓
- Flowers for Louise ✓
- See Sally about chairs

Step 5   At the end of the day (or the start of the next day), add to your new 'To Do' list the tasks which have not been done. Look at your continuous master list and transfer Immediate items to your 'To Do' list and Future items to your diary:

To do Thurs 5 Sept.
- See Jean re Marshall Bros (from previous 'To Do')
- See Sally about chairs (from previous 'To Do')
- Ring Sam – 0181 339 3681 – re transfer of lease (from master)
- See Lynn re Brian's appraisal (from master)
- Collect air tickets (from master)
- Book car in for a service (from master)

In order to work, your 'To Do' list must be:

- written – 'out of sight, out of mind'. If tasks aren't written down it's easy to forget and lose track of what needs to be done
- updated every single day – **without fail**.

PRIORITIZING TASKS

Individual tasks need to be prioritized so that the most urgent and important are attended to first. Each objective or task will fall into one of the following categories:

- Urgent and important: A key management task which is closely related to a important objective, and which has a fast approaching deadline.
- Important but not urgent: A key management task which is closely related to a important objective.
- Urgent but not important: A task which has a fast approaching deadline.
- Neither important nor urgent: A task which is not closely related to a high-level objective and which does not have a fast approaching deadline.

Which are your top three time wasters?

Time wasters are those activities:

- in which we consciously become involved
- in which other people involve us.

The next activity will give you a chance to think about the three main time wasters which steal your time away.

ACTIVITY 24

List three activities which most often waste time for you at work and then, alongside each time waster you have identified, note down what you have to do to manage the time waster.

1 Time waster:
How I take control of this time waster:

2 Time waster:
How I take control of this time waster:

3 Time waster:
How I take control of this time waster:

FEEDBACK

There are many time wasters which you might have identified, including:

- unexpected visitors to your office
- telephone calls that seem to last forever
- conversations that go round in circles
- meetings that start late, finish late and achieve nothing
- getting drawn into situations you would prefer to avoid (but don't know how to get out of)
- procrastination and indecision.

UNEXPECTED VISITORS TO YOUR OFFICE

Having an 'open-door' policy will benefit everyone except you. People, knowing that your door is always open, will pop along to see you **when it suits them**. Once you've committed yourself to an open-door policy it's very difficult to say to people: 'I'm glad you came to see me... but I'm too busy to talk to you now.' The best way to deal with unexpected visitors is to block out periods of time when you do have an 'open door'. These times might be, say, every morning 8.30–9.30 or Monday, Wednesday and Friday 3.00–5.00 or whenever it suits you best. The key to successfully implementing this kind of strategy is to let people know the **days** and **times** when you **are** available. Also, fully brief your secretary so that she can clearly judge whether or not the situation is sufficiently serious to warrant allowing an unexpected visitor to see you. If you don't have a secretary, make a mutually beneficial deal with a colleague. Agree that you will do 'guard duty' for him if he will reciprocate for you. Visitors, when confronted by someone else, will quickly get the message that you really are not available. If there's no other way around it and unexpected visitors do drop in:

- stand up and don't invite your visitor to sit down
- greet them politely, but let them know they can have just five minutes
- if it becomes obvious that the reason for the visit is complex and clearly needs more than five minutes, set an appointment when you can get together and give the matter due consideration.

TELEPHONE CALLS THAT SEEM TO LAST FOREVER

Before you make a telephone call, note down your objective (what you want to achieve) and your core statement, as discussed in Section 2 of this workbook.

Use assertiveness skills to draw the conversation back to the main topic, your objective and your core statement. Don't be afraid to end the call with a simple and courteous statement like, for example, 'Well, you've given me a lot to think about, Harry. It's been really good to talk to you and I'll get back to you within a day or so.'

CONVERSATIONS THAT GO ROUND IN CIRCLES

Again, stick to your objective and your core statement. If it seems as though the conversation is going nowhere, end courteously and assertively. In situations like this, the key point to remember is that even though the other person doesn't mind wasting **his** time, he has no right to waste **your** time.

MEETINGS THAT START LATE, FINISH LATE AND ACHIEVE NOTHING

Lengthy and mismanaged meetings are a tremendous waste of time. There are a number of key steps you can take to ensure that meetings are productive.

- **If you are attending the meeting**:
  - before you go, make sure you have all the documents you might need
  - confirm with the Chair the date and place of the meeting, and the start and finish times. Make it clear that you have another follow-on appointment and that you will not be available to stay past the anticipated finish time
  - arrive on time
  - acknowledge colleagues and friends, by all means, but be ready to start at the appointed time
  - focus on the items on the agenda and don't waste time by going off at a tangent, or introducing unexpected side issues. You are there to deal with the business in hand
  - listen carefully and contribute your views and opinions
  - at the agreed finishing time gather your papers, remind the Chair that you have another appointment, and leave.

- **If you are chairing the meeting**:
  - start on time
  - keep the discussion focused on the relevant issues
  - encourage people to contribute, ask questions, summarize what has been said or agreed. Prod the group to make a decision. Keep things moving
  - keep a careful eye on the clock and end the meeting on time.

GETTING DRAWN INTO SITUATIONS YOU WOULD PREFER TO AVOID (BUT DON'T KNOW HOW TO GET OUT OF)

This happens to everyone from time to time until they learn how to say 'No'.

The key point to remember is that when you say no **you are simply refusing the request, and not rejecting the person**. Every time you agree to do something you know you don't want to do, just think about how much time you will be wasting.

PROCRASTINATION AND INDECISION

We are all familiar with that sinking feeling that comes from looking at a task which involves a great deal of work, and is either complex and difficult, or boring and uninspiring. In these circumstances, it's often tempting to push the task to the bottom of the pile and focus attention on something which is smaller, more interesting, enjoyable and worthwhile. The problem is that the big, complex/boring job doesn't go away. One day, usually when you least feel able to cope with it, it becomes big, complex/boring and very, very urgent. Faced with a task which you really don't want to do, make a commitment to yourself that you will make a start, and then spend some time working on it every day, or even every week. Even a twenty-page report, completed at the rate of two pages per day, will get done in two weeks. Once you start, you might even find that you enjoy it. The key things to remember are:

- Don't put things off because they appear to be 'too big' or 'too difficult'
- Don't always do the easy or the enjoyable tasks first. You'll soon find (surprise, surprise) that there isn't time to do the other stuff
- Plan ahead, prioritize and work to your 'To Do' list.

Paperwork

Most managers struggle with a mountain of paperwork, which usually consists of letters, memos, reports, quotations, estimates and/or proposals. The keys to managing paper are:

- Deal with it, or
- Delegate it, or
- Dump it.

DEAL WITH IT

Time management experts all agree that the best way to handle incoming paper is to deal with each item only once. So when you look at your daily post you should decide whether to deal with it yourself, delegate it to someone else or dump it.

Many of the documents to which you will need to respond will require a *standard* reply. A good time-saver is to prepare a set of standard letters. For example:

- Thanks for your letter, I'll get back to you (A1)
- Thanks for the invitation, I'll be there (A2)
- Yes, I'd like to (A3)
- No, I don't want to (B1)
- Please pay now (B2)
- Please stop sending me junk mail (B3)

and so on. If your secretary has a set of standard letters, all you need do is to write on each piece of paper (the letter or memo or report you've received) the standard response you would like her to prepare. This will save a great deal of time which can then be devoted to writing or dictating mail which is not standard and which needs an individual approach.

DELEGATE IT

Of course, there will be many items of paperwork which require your personal attention. But do think about which items can be delegated to other people. For instance, if a report arrives on your desk which is not **really** relevant or important but which **might** contain useful information or statistics, pass it on to someone else (your secretary or a junior colleague), tell them the kind of information you want and ask them to read it for you. You can also do this with magazines, journals and newspaper articles.

DUMP IT

Don't be tempted to shuffle papers around or store them in a 'For Later' paper basket. 'Later' never comes. Be ruthless. Ask yourself: 'Can I deal with this?', 'Can I delegate this?', even 'If I never saw this again, would I miss it, and would it matter?'

When looking at ways to improve your time management, do remember Murphy's Ten Laws of Time Management, taken from Patrick Forsyth's book *First Things First*[1].

1 *If anything can go wrong, it will do so*
2 *Nothing is ever as simple as it seems*
3 *If you mess with something for long enough, it will break*
4 *If you try to please everybody, somebody won't like it*
5 *Nothing ever works out exactly as you expect*
6 *Whatever you want to do, there is always something else you have to do first*
7 *If you explain something so that no-one could possibly misunderstand, someone will*
8 *Nothing is certain until it has happened (and then you should check it more than once)*
9 *If everything goes according to plan, then it is a sure sign that something is about to go wrong*
10 *The only predictable thing about your day is that something totally unexpected will happen.*

Use the next activity as an opportunity to create a meaningful action plan to help you take control of your time.

ACTIVITY 25

1a   Begin by identifying four practical things you can do to help you take control of your time:

    1

    2

    3

    4

1b   Note down the date when you intend to put these ideas into action.
Start date:

1c   Note down the date when you plan to review progress.
Review date:

2a   On the review date (see 1c above), note down your answers to the following questions:

■   What success have you achieved with your time management strategy? What has worked well (i.e. saved time), and what has not worked well?

■   What (if anything) will you do differently in the future?

Learning summary

1. At work you have four different kinds of time-slots available to you:
    - fixed time-slots (for regular activities such as meetings which occur at specific, fixed times)
    - flexible time-slots (for routine activities such as correspondence, phone calls, meetings, networking and so on)
    - personal time-slots (for working on your own projects, e.g. reports or data collection)
    - Unexpected time-slots (which occur because of cancellations)
2. The key to successful time management is:
    - planning ahead and allocating parts of the working week to fixed time, flexible time and personal time activities
    - preparing a list of activities which you can usefully work through when unexpected time presents itself
3. Managing your diary by:
    - using a pencil
    - noting details as well as names
    - setting a time limit (start and finish times) will save time
4. Your master list is a continuous list of **every single thing** you have to do. Add items to your master list as they crop up
5. At the end or beginning of each day, consult your master list and:
    - transfer future items to your diary
    - transfer current items to your 'To Do' list
    - tick each item on your 'To Do' list as soon as it is done
    - at the end or beginning of the day, transfer any items which have not been done to your new 'To Do' list
    - consult your master list and repeat the process
6. Prioritize each item on your 'To Do' list and do the most urgent and important things first. Don't do the easy and enjoyable things first
7. The three key steps to tackling paperwork are:
    - deal with it, or
    - delegate it, or
    - dump it

Reference

1   Forsyth, Patrick (1994) *First things First*, Institute of Management and Pitman Publishing, page 11.

Section 5   The relationship manager

Introduction

Your ability to create good working relationships with colleagues will have a direct bearing on how well you work with them. The better the relationship, the more likely you are to work effectively together.

Within any organization there will be people with whom you get along really well and people with whom you have a fairly neutral relationship. There may also be others with whom you have a difficult relationship. You will increase your success as a manager if you can:

- increase the number of good working relationships
- convert the neutral to good
- decrease the number of difficult relationships by converting them to neutral.

How people relate to you all depends on your behaviour. No one can read your mind, so other people will interpret your behaviour (i.e. what you do and say) and act accordingly. For example:

If they interpret your behaviour as...	People will respond by ...
someone who: - is fair, reasonable and honest - has a genuine concern for other view people's feelings and point of view	... being prepared to listen to and respect your point of view and requests
someone who: - is arrogant, unreasonable and economical with the truth - has little regard for other people's opinions or concerns	... being unwilling to listen or respect what you have to say

In this section we look at some of the ingredients of good working relationships and their associated behaviours. They include:

- empathy
- being open
- trust
- respecting diversity.

It gives you an opportunity to consider how other people perceive you and check that your behaviour is a true reflection of what you want to convey.

Empathy

Empathy is about sensing a person's unspoken feelings and concerns and then responding appropriately to them. It involves being able to see things from someone else's point of view rather than making assumptions about what they think. If you are empathetic it sends out clear messages to people that you are interested in them and value them – foundations for any good relationship.

Being empathetic involves a combination of:

- listening
- picking up clues from body language.

Listening

Nature gave us one tongue and two ears so we could hear twice as much as we speak.
Epictetus

Listening is a skill. It's an active process which involves:

- focusing on what someone else is saying
- banishing your own agenda from your mind
- being non-judgemental
- not making assumptions.

By really listening to what someone is saying you send a clear message that you value them – that they are important enough for you to spend time listening to them.

In addition, a good listener does not simply absorb everything that is said without comment, but helps the speaker to articulate and explain his or her ideas by:

- **Being encouraging.** When you want a speaker to tell you more, it can be useful to prompt them occasionally with a simple 'Yes', 'Right', or 'Mmm'. You will often find that people pause slightly to let you make signals like this.
- **Allowing silence.** It can be productive to wait for the person talking to gather their thoughts and continue instead of jumping in to fill a silence.
- **Paraphrasing or summarizing.** This is a way of checking that you understand what is being said. It involves repeating the essence of what has been said in your own words. It shows the speaker that you have been listening and may enable them to clarify their thoughts.
- **Reflecting.** This is similar to paraphrasing. It involves echoing the last part of what has been said in your own words.

    A: The trouble is, Sally was absolutely brilliant with the customers and I'm finding it very hard to find a replacement of the same calibre.

    B: Someone with similar skills.

    A: That's right. I mean, Sally really was quite unique.
- **Referring to things said earlier.** If you can remember and repeat things that people have said earlier it shows you have not only listened but also taken in and remembered it.

Few people, if any, are good listeners all of the time. However, you need to be aware that by not listening to someone you are sending out the distinct message that what they have to say isn't important to you.

ACTIVITY 26

Think of someone – either a colleague or someone you know outside work – whom you always enjoy talking to. Which of the following statements are true?

		True	False
1	Things often seem a lot clearer after I've spoken to him/her.	❏	❏
2	He/she always seems interested in what I've got to say.	❏	❏
3	He/she is so entertaining, I don't have to contribute much to the conversation.	❏	❏
4	I find it easy to explain things to him/her.	❏	❏
5	He/she is very quick at picking things up.	❏	❏

FEEDBACK

You probably decided that all of the statements, apart from number 3, are true. The conversations we enjoy most are those in which we feel that our contribution is heard and understood by the other person. You may find it useful to consider whether someone else would tick the same boxes about you.

Picking up clues from body language

You can often tell more about what somebody is thinking or really means by watching their body language, e.g. amount of eye contact, facial expressions, body posture. Experts estimate that 55–80% of meaning is conveyed through body language when we communicate.

Mortals can keep no secret. If their lips are silent, they gossip with their fingertips; betrayal forces its way through every pore.

Sigmund Freud

We can read a lot into what someone else is feeling by observing their body language. It's an innate skill. However, people vary as to how much they develop and use the skill. It involves focusing your thoughts on the other person's body language rather than being too busy to pick up all but the very obvious signals.

ACTIVITY 27

You will need a friend or colleague to help you with this activity. During a conversation, practise using body language to indicate that you:

1 are very interested in what the other person is saying
2 want to move on to another topic
3 are very bored with listening to the other person.

Take turns at listening and speaking. Then answer these questions.

■ How did it feel to be on the receiving end of these signals?

■ Which techniques were most effective?

FEEDBACK

The more conscious you become about body language, the more you will be able to pick up signals from other people. You may also find it useful to observe the body language of people around you when you are next in a pub or on a train. Just by observing, see how much you can pick up about what other people are feeling. Discreet observation of other people is an excellent way to improve your own sensitivity to body language.

Developing your empathy skills takes up relatively little time. Once they become a habit they take up even less time as you'll do it almost unconsciously. However, it can bring enormous benefits to the quality of relationships you have with the people around you.

Being open

People around you will feel more comfortable if you are open about what you think. But being open is not just about letting others know where you stand. Plenty of people are all too ready to make their points of view known to others! It's also about encouraging others to be open with you by listening to them so you can also see things from their point of view. So, being open involves:

- keeping people informed about what's happening, *and* answering any concerns or questions honestly
- letting people know what you think and feel, *and* listening to what others think and feel
- sharing your opinions, *and* seeking out the opinions of others.

The Johari Window, so called as it was developed by Joe Luft and Harry Ingham in the 1950s, looks at aspects of how open we are with other people. The model consists of a four-box grid as shown below.

	Known to self	Unknown to self
Known to others	*Box 1* Known to self and others: *Public area*	*Box 3* Unknown to self but known to others: *Blind area*
Unknown to others	*Box 2* Known to self but not to others: *Hidden area*	*Box 4* Not known to self or others: *Unknown area*

Box 1 in the grid represents those areas of a person's personality which are openly known and acknowledged by the person and people around, i.e. the public area. Box 2 represents areas of personality that are deliberately not shared with others – they're kept hidden. Box 3 represents areas which are known to others but we don't recognise in ourselves. Finally, Box 4, the 'unknown area' represents areas which are not known to others or to yourself.

ACTIVITY 28

What is likely to happen to the size of Box A in relation to the other quadrants if:

- you are at ease with others around you?

- you are in new company, an unfamiliar situation?

FEEDBACK

When you feel at ease with people around you, Box A is likely to enlarge. You'll be more relaxed and less likely to hide your thoughts and feelings. Conversely, in an unfamiliar situation Box A is likely to be smaller and Box B bigger.

It's important to be aware of Box 3, the blind area. As we highlighted when looking at empathy, you are continually sending out messages through what you do and say.

Sometimes being open may seem risky as you may not feel comfortable trusting other people with your thoughts and feelings. However, people who interact with others through a 'small' Box A often have difficulty forming good relationships.

Trust

According to Douglas McGregor trust is, *'the knowledge that you will not deliberately or accidentally, consciously or unconsciously take advantage of me'.*

There are two sides to trust within a relationship. There can be:

- trustworthy behaviour (i.e. responding to trust others place in you)
- trusting behaviour (i.e. putting your trust in others).

There should be no instances when you don't display trustworthy behaviour. It involves:

- not betraying confidences
- communicating – keep people informed
- keeping promises
- being honest
- not misleading people
- admitting when you are wrong
- showing concern for others.

Putting your trust in someone else involves being vulnerable to the response of another person. It can be risky and many people, who find that their trust has been misplaced, will be more reluctant to trust in the future.

As a manager you have to trust people in your team, e.g. when you delegate. Until you know the person very well, it often involves a degree of risk but you can often mimimize the risk with adequate support.

I knew Rashid wanted to represent the department at the monthly route meeting and that it would free up my time if he could go instead of me. It was an important meeting because we were bidding for funding. Anyhow I talked about it with Rashid and he was keen to go ahead. We decided that we'd get together beforehand and go through all the arguments in detail. Rashid would then put together the proposal and I'd give him feedback on his presentation before he went along to the meeting.

It all turned out well. His presentation was excellent; all the facts and figures researched in great detail. We got the funding and Rashid's confidence was given a real boost.

ACTIVITY 29

Identify one occasion when you trusted someone at work and the trust proved to be well-founded. Then think of an instance when you feel your trust was misplaced.

Why do you think the two occasions had different outcomes?

FEEDBACK

It could have been lack of preparation on your part; equally the behaviour on the part of the other person may have been inexcusable.

Absence of trust is a feature of many poor relationships. Where you recognize that to be the case, try to develop trust by:

■ always showing trustworthy behaviour yourself
■ identifying situations where you can show trusting behaviour – most people respond eventually!

Respecting diversity

It's human nature to feel at ease with the attitudes and ways of doing things that you are used to. You will select your friends on the basis of who you feel comfortable with, and there's nothing wrong with that.

However, difficulties can arise if people think that others should behave and look at the world in the same way as they do themselves … and that if they don't, then they are in some way 'not normal' or 'wrong'. Recognizing that other people have values, beliefs and ways of doing things that are different but of *equal value* is an important step to make for anyone. In your role as a manager it's essential if you are to benefit from the diverse ideas, viewpoints and skills that a range of people from a wide variety of backgrounds can bring.

Although in theory it sounds obvious, in practice it can be harder to do. We all grow up in an individual culture which shapes our values, beliefs and ultimately attitudes. We assume that our own values and beliefs are 'right'; we have to in order to operate as human beings. However, if the beliefs and values on which you base your attitudes are unfounded or incomplete then your attitudes would be flawed and, consequently, the basis on which you build relationships with other people.

ACTIVITY 30

Consider the following statements. What do you think?

1 Disability is the inability to perform an action and is caused by the impairment (e.g. being blind, deaf). WHO (1980)

2 Disability is caused by the way society is organized – people don't give thought to the needs of people with impairments when they design things. That's what causes disability. (UPIAS – Union of Physically Impaired Against Segregation)

FEEDBACK

Your views are likely to have been shaped by your life experiences and they will affect your attitude towards recruiting staff with disability. For example, agreeing with the first statement and dismissing the second will probably make you less likely to explore or recognize adjustments that can be made to integrate a person with a disability into the workplace.

What's important is that you constantly challenge your attitudes and ask yourself questions such as:

- What makes me think that?
- How is that influencing my behaviour?
- What evidence do I have?
- What other ways are there of looking at it?

Try to be more objective in your approach by looking at facts, rather than your long-held beliefs, if you think that:

■   you are being influenced by stereotypical beliefs and attitudes about people (i.e. beliefs based on the characteristics of a group of people instead of their individual capabilities), or
■   you have a narrow view of what is 'acceptable' or 'normal'.

In other words, it's about proactively challenging any prejudices which you may unintentionally have developed.

Reflecting on your relationship skills

The way we interact with other people is very personal; there is no blueprint for an effective working relationship. However, reflecting on your behaviour can provide a valuable insight into how other people perceive you and give you the opportunity to change, if necessary.

ACTIVITY 31

Choose a person at work with whom you have a 'difficult' or 'neutral' relationship.

How do you think that person perceives you?

Consider the aspects of relationships covered in this section. In your opinion, would it benefit the relationships if either or both of you focused on one or more aspect?

	Yourself	Other person
Empathy	❏	❏
Being open	❏	❏
Trusting behaviour	❏	❏
Trustworthy behaviour	❏	❏
Respecting diversity	❏	❏

What practical steps could you take to try and improve the relationship?

FEEDBACK

It is essential to recognise that:

- other people will judge you on the basis on your behaviour
- the way you behave will have a direct impact on the way other people behave towards you.

Learning summary

1 Some of the ingredients of a good working relationship include empathy, being open, trust and respecting diversity

2 Empathy is about sensing a person's unspoken feelings and concerns. It involves:
- listening
- picking up clues from body language
- responding appropriately.

3 Being open involves:
- keeping people informed about what's happening, *and* answering any concerns or questions honestly
- letting people know what you think and feel, *and* listening to what others think and feel
- sharing your opinions, *and* seeking out the opinions of others.

4 There are two sides to trust within any relationship:
- trustworthy behaviour (i.e. responding to trust others place in you)
- trusting behaviour (i.e. putting your trust in others).

5 Valuing diversity involves:
- acceptance that we all feel comfortable with the way we do things, i.e. our own culture *but* the norms of other people are of equal value
- challenging any prejudices we have.

6 Other people will judge you on the basis on your behaviour.

7 The way you behave will have a direct impact on the way other people behave towards you.

Reference

1   McGregor, D (1987) *The Human Side of Enterprise*, Penguin.

Section 6   The conflict manager

Introduction

It is not unusual to hear managers muttering, in the privacy of their car or office, 'This job would be great if it wasn't for the people!' If you have ever uttered these words in a moment of despair, and subsequently felt guilty, don't worry – you're not alone.

Regardless of the type of organization for which you work, one of your key roles will be managing other people. You will also, probably, belong to one or more teams, as a team member. This means that, on a daily basis, there will be countless opportunities for you to either become embroiled in conflict with other people, or have to deal with the conflict which has occurred between other people. The conflicts may be fairly minor – for instance, someone insists on regularly parking in your allocated space, or someone persists in making sarcastic and unprofessional remarks about your ability to do the job. Or they may be potentially very serious – for example, two of your team members become involved in physical violence in the company car park, or team members complain that a colleague is unable to work safely because of substance abuse.

If you are really lucky you may, on average, find yourself having to sort out some kind of conflict once or twice a week. If you are like most managers, then dealing with conflict is a regular, daily occurrence for you. Whether you are personally involved, or merely sorting things out between other people, conflict management will almost certainly affect you, one way or another. Most managers find that, as conflict at work increases, their own stress levels rise. This is often because dealing with the conflict takes up so much time that they have great difficulty in meeting their own job description and achieving their own objectives.

In this section of the workbook we shall be looking at the most common causes of conflict and the action you can take to manage those situations effectively.

What causes conflict at work?

The main *root* causes of conflict are:

- success
- objectives and beliefs
- territory
- irrational hostility
- personal style.

The next activity will give you an opportunity to think about those occasions when you have been drawn into conflict because of these root causes.

ACTIVITY 32

1 Cast your mind back to an occasion in your working life when you were obviously successful and your success was, in some way, recognized and rewarded.

(a) How did your managers, colleagues and subordinates perceive your success?

(b) In what way did your success affect your working relationships?

(c) Were there any negative responses? If so, what were they?

(d) What was the effect of your success on your subsequent job performance?

(e) What was the final outcome?

2 Think back to a time in your working life when either your objectives or your beliefs have been in conflict with those of your managers, colleagues or subordinates.

   (a) How did you perceive those people whose objectives or beliefs were in conflict with yours?

   (b) To the best of your knowledge, how did they perceive you?

   (c) How did this conflict affect the job performance of everyone involved?

   (d) What was the final outcome?

3 When was the last time you were involved in conflict over territory – e.g. parking space, office space or furniture, equipment, budget allocation or other resources?

   (a) What was the territory which caused the conflict?

   (b) Did you feel that someone was stepping on your territory? Or did someone else think you were invading theirs?

   (c) What was the outcome?

4 When was the last time you objected to someone at work for a trivial reason? (Maybe their appearance or mannerisms, or perhaps a casual remark to which you took exception.)

   (a) What was the cause of your hostility to this person? Was it something they did? Or said? Or the way they looked? Something else?

(b) How did your hostility manifest itself? How did you behave? How did you communicate?

(c) Did you ever get over the hostility and resolve the conflict? What was the final outcome?

5 Review the conflict situations in which you have been involved and think about how differences in personal style may have been a contributing factor.

(a) What differences of personal style were involved (e.g. Outgoing and charismatic v Plodding and painstaking)?

(b) Would the conflict have occurred if the differences in personal style had not existed?

(c) Is there a pattern? For example, are there certain types of people with whom you tend to come into conflict?

FEEDBACK

SUCCESS AS A CAUSE OF CONFLICT

Some UK, and many US, companies encourage an atmosphere of healthy competition where *success* is cheerfully recognized and **genuinely** celebrated. In these organizations people who do well are respected, and their contributions are highly valued. Unfortunately, in many UK companies, success – and the energy, drive, ambition and hard work which are the main contributing factors for success – are often viewed in a rather different light. UK managers sometimes perceive successful colleagues as a threat. Success can lead to jealousy and resentment, and these negative attitudes can lead to considerable discord. Cliques and subgroups can form, consisting of the 'successful' people, and the people who perceive themselves as 'less successful'. Discord can grow into conflict and even, on occasion, turn into a major war between individuals, teams, departments, functions or units of the same company located in different parts of the country. Diana, a conference manager in the hotel industry, explains how her personal success at work caused conflict:

I work for a multinational organization which has hotel and leisure facilities all over the world. About three years ago the company ran a 'suggestions promotion', and the idea was that the person who came up with the best suggestions for improving customer service would be rewarded with an international tour of our flagship properties. I won the trip and went to Hong Kong, Singapore and the States on a working holiday. It was fabulous, and I learned a lot and, of course, came back full of new ideas. I was shocked and very upset to discover the amount of hostility I had to deal with. People with whom I had worked well with **before** *the trip changed dramatically in their attitudes and levels of co-operation* **after** *the trip. Instead of people being pleased for me, and being open to new possibilities for the business, there was petty jealousy and open hostility. It was a very difficult time for me and, although I did manage to stick it out, there were many times I felt like looking around for another job.'*

OBJECTIVES AND BELIEFS AS A SOURCE OF CONFLICT

Within every organization you can expect to find a group of people with different *views, opinions, beliefs* and different personal and work-related *objectives.* This is both healthy and desirable because it leads to a continuous exchange of ideas, an atmosphere of creative competition and an often unspoken 'agreement to disagree'. But different ways of looking at the same task or concept can provide fertile ground for conflict:

- Sylvia's role is to set and control budgets and to make sure that spending stays within the agreed allocations. Mike feels that her approach is too rigid, and her refusal to fund additional resources for his department has, in the long term, cost the company a considerable amount of money. Outcome: **conflict**
- In his spare time Neal is an active member of Greenpeace. He believes passionately in the preservation of the environment and clashes, head-on, with his MD who refuses to sanction more expensive but more environmentally aware working practices. Outcome: **conflict**
- Tim likes to think of himself as a 'New Man' who treats everyone equally and who is perfectly happy to make his secretary a cup of tea. Arthur, Tim's colleague, likes to think of himself as 'one of the lads' and can't see the point of 'all this equal opportunities nonsense'. Outcome: **conflict**

TERRITORY AS A SOURCE OF CONFLICT

Perfectly sane, intelligent and responsible people can lose all sense of proportion when they feel that their territory is being invaded. *Territory* can mean personal space – for instance, an office, a chair, a parking space – but can also mean:

- time
- resources (budget allocations, equipment, staffing)
- pay (salary, overtime, bonus, commission)

- job-related 'perks' (expense account (sandwiches or decent lunch in a good restaurant), car (diesel family saloon or top-of-the-range high-performance vehicle), quality of accommodation and travel (three-star or five-star hotel: Economy or Business Class), staff (part-time agency temp or full-time graduate personal assistant), communications (phone card or digital mobile phone), technology [basic PC with limited usage or state-of-the-art multi-media with accessories])
- responsibilities
- preferred status relationships with important clients or senior management within the company.

IRRATIONAL HOSTILITY AS A SOURCE OF CONFLICT

If you are like most people, there will have been times in your life when you have taken an instant dislike to someone, or you've had a deep-seated resistance to doing something. If closely questioned, you wouldn't have been able to give a logical reason for your response. You might have muttered, 'He looks shifty', or 'I don't think she's got her mind on the job', or 'He reminds me of my old headmaster' or 'I don't like the sound of the project – It just doesn't feel right.'

Any one of these views could reasonably be described as an *irrational hostility*. They arise out of our perceptions of other people (which can often be wrong) and they colour our feelings towards them:

- Jim reminds you of your headmaster. You didn't have a good relationship with your headmaster. You didn't like him, and the feeling was mutual. Jim's resemblance triggers off unhappy memories, and you make the connection (probably erroneously) that the headmaster was like this, so Jim will probably be like this, too!

The key point to remember is that, from time to time, you may feel irrationally hostile towards some people; and others may have these feelings too. They may 'take against' you or other colleagues for no real reason. Irrational hostility, which usually has no real logical or sensible foundation, can often be found at the core of conflict.

PERSONAL STYLE AS A SOURCE OF CONFLICT

Personal style is an amalgamation of attitudes, perceptions, style of communication, personality, habits and ways of doing things. Many leading-edge management thinkers have created systems for dividing people into different types, categories, behaviours and operational styles. Examples of these include:

- learning styles
- management styles
- team roles
- personality.

You will come across a number of these in some of the other workbooks. In the meantime, use Figure 6.1 as a rough guide to help you to see how conflict can easily arise between people who have different personal styles.

TRADITIONALISTS	ANALYSTS
■ prefer familiar, safe situations ■ creatures of habit ■ like to have routines and established systems and procedures ■ like to form close, often social, relationships with other team members ■ generally predictable, patient and loyal	■ slow at decision making because they need to analyse, think things through and explore all the options ■ high standards, both for themselves and the other team members ■ generally thoughtful, precise, systematic and highly critical
COMPETITORS	PERFORMERS
■ easily bored by routine ■ motivated by the possibility of success ■ because they thrive on change, are keen to experiment and find new ways of doing things ■ make decisions quickly and easily, and enjoy risk-taking and the thrill of the chase ■ generally confident, impatient, ambitious people who like to get the job done and move on to the next challenge	■ extremely sociable and good with people, they love to charm, persuade and convince ■ prefer people to systems or ideas ■ can be impulsive and often take a slapdash 'it'll be all right on the night' approach ■ generally optimistic, easy-going, enthusiastic and fun

Figure 6.1

ACTIVITY 33

Examine Figure 6.1 and note down, in the space below, four areas of conflict which could arise between the four different personal styles; Traditionalists, Analysts, Competitors and Performers.

1

2

3

4

In any situation which involved a mix of these four personal styles, there would be numerous opportunities for conflict, such as:

- Competitors would be keen to get on with making the decision (possibly any decision, just as long as **something** was decided), while the Analysts would want to look at the problem from all angles. Performers wouldn't really care too much about the decision-making process because they really want to get out and about, where the action is. The Traditionalists would be worried that the decision might mean change, and change is difficult for them to deal with.
- Performers are generally optimistic and easy-going and not overly concerned with detail, while Analysts want things to be **right** – and to get things right, you have to do things properly. Competitors are good at initiating but not necessarily good at completing, so any hold-ups (to get things right) would be a source of frustration and irritation.
- Traditionalists like to get on well with people, and so do Performers. But Competitors are more interested in forging ahead with new ideas, and don't really have time for unnecessary socializing.
- Traditionalists are steady and hard-working; Competitors are dynamic and hard-working.
- Performers are people-orientated and they shine in a social setting, whereas Analysts are systems-orientated people who prefer ideas to people.
- Competitors are often addicted to adrenalin and, when things are too quiet, they will proactively look for challenging new horizons. Traditionalists prefer to stick with what they know, and feel uncomfortable with changing goalposts.

As someone who will be called upon, from time to time, to manage conflict it is important that you understand how differences in personal style can be the main trigger for interpersonal difficulties. Conflict may arise not because people are being intentionally difficult (although this sometimes can be the case), but just because they are looking at the same picture down different ends of the telescope, seeing the same thing from widely differing points of view.

Symptoms and tactics

Clearly, before you can attempt to resolve conflict you need to be aware that the conflict exists. Sometimes there are overt symptoms and tactics such as:

- **symptom**: breakdown in communication
- **tactic**: written complaint about the 'other party' to union or health and safety representative or senior management.

Sometimes the symptoms and tactics are much more subtle. Figure 6.2 identifies the main symptoms of conflict and the tactics which people tend to use in an attempt to 'win'.

Symptoms	Tactics
■ **Communication** – arguments, fights and tears – excessive politeness and formality – cessation of communication – proliferation of memos and other paperwork – frosty, tense atmosphere – request for intervention by senior management ■ **Deterioration in work standards** – missed targets – non-attendance at meetings – clock-watching – low morale – lack of co-operation without sound reason	■ **Communication** – distorting the facts by giving one person, team or department one story, and other people an entirely different version ■ **Red tape** – tying people in knots with red tape so that it becomes extremely difficult for them to do their job ('I want a detailed activity report on my desk every morning') ■ **Bypassing official channels** – manipulating people in key positions to provide information or authorization ('Ted's already authorized it, so there's nothing for you to do') ■ **Subtle sabotage** – making sure that errors and indiscretions (or even untruths) are passed on to the right people ('Tania works too hard ... and of course since she's had the baby she's just so tired all the time ...')

Figure 6.2 Symptoms of conflict, and the tactics adversaries use in order to 'win'

Trouble-shooting

The bad news is that, as a manager, as soon as you become aware of hostilities – whether directed towards you or another member of your team – it is your responsibility to do something about it. The good news is that if you take the initiative and act promptly and assertively, you can nip it in the bud and prevent a minor conflict from developing into a major crisis.

ACTIVITY 34

Read through the following case studies and note down, for each: (a) two strategies you should avoid when dealing with these situations and (b) two strategies you could use to resolve the situations.

CASE STUDY 1

You feel that a colleague (a manager from another function who is on the same grade as yourself) is undermining your position at work. Although there isn't much that you can specifically put your finger on, comments have been made by two members of your team to the effect that this colleague has criticized your ideas and the way in which you are managing an important project. Your MD has also made a couple of remarks, which suggest to you that your colleague has been using subtle sabotage to raise doubts about your competence. What are you going to do about it?

(a) Strategies I should avoid when dealing with this situation:

(b) Strategies I could use to resolve this situation:

CASE STUDY 2

Josie, a member of your team, complains to you that Nicholas, another member of the team, is consistently providing incorrect data in the reports he submits to her on a monthly basis. She suggests to you that the inaccuracies are deliberately designed to cause problems for her and increase her workload. You are aware that there has previously been some subtle tension between these two team members. What are you going to do about it?

(a)   Strategies I should avoid when dealing with this situation:

(b)   Strategies I could use to resolve this situation:

CASE STUDY 3

Your CEO is planning to move the factory to an out-of-town Greenfield site. She invites you to a one-to-one meeting and explains that just about everyone in the organization is vigorously resisting the move. She asks you to talk to the staff and the union representatives in order to 'get them to see sense.'

(a)   Strategies I should avoid when dealing with this situation:

(b)   Strategies I could use to resolve this situation:

FEEDBACK

CASE STUDY 1

This is quite a delicate situation because, at this stage, you don't have any real evidence. You have second-hand information provided by your team members (which may or may not be a distortion of the truth), and a couple of chance remarks made by the MD (to which you may well be over-reacting). In these circumstances, strategies to **avoid** include the following:

Confrontation

If, as is often the case, this scenario has been blown up out of all proportion by **other people**, by confronting your colleague you could appear to be insecure (at best) and totally paranoid (at worst).

Collusion or collaboration

Never be tempted to ask other people to gossip or gather evidence on your behalf. Comments like 'Keep your ear to the ground and let me know if he says anything else' are extremely unprofessional. They also have a nasty habit of backfiring.

Retaliation

Just because **you have been told** or **you think** that someone is using subtle sabotage against you is no excuse for responding in similar fashion.

Strategies to **use** include the following:

Watchfulness

Be careful and cautious around this person, and behave, at all times, with the utmost professionalism. Give this person no cause whatsoever to criticize you or your actions. Say nothing, even as a joke, which you would not be happy to have repeated to your MD (or anyone else).

Assertiveness

Behave assertively at all times with this person. Let them see that you are not a soft touch, and that you are comfortable voicing your views and opinions clearly, and with confidence. Let them know, through words and actions, that, in your view, back-biting, rumour-mongering, gossip and good, old-fashioned lies are unethical and unprofessional.

If you do manage to get some concrete evidence — a memo, letter, e-mail, specific comments made in your presence — then act immediately. Keep your temper and ask coolly and calmly for an explanation: 'I notice that you seem to think that I've been mismanaging the Morgan project. I find that very interesting, and I'd like to know more.' If the person involved tries to bluster or bluff, then you can pin them down and assertively ask for details: 'I'd really like to know, specifically, in what way you think I'm mismanaging the project.'

The key point here is that it is often much easier to resolve conflict **between other people** than it is to deal with conflict **between yourself and someone else**. This is because, where others are involved, as a manager you will have very little emotional involvement in the situation. Of course, you will want a speedy resolution so that you can restore harmony and normal working practices, and get the people involved off your back. When you are personally involved, however, things can be very different. Your emotions are likely to be stirred up, and you may feel:

- angry
- humiliated
- highly competitive and determined to win, or even spiteful and malicious towards the other person, ('You're trying to hurt me, so here's a taste of your own medicine').

Retaliation will not help, as it will only serve to escalate the conflict and, in the long run, make matters worse. So what can you do if you find yourself in direct conflict with someone else?

1   **Look for the root cause of the conflict**. The real, underlying reason for the conflict between you and someone else will probably be either success, objectives and beliefs, territory, irrational hostility or personal style.
2   **Deal with the root cause**. Some suggestions as to how you might do this are outlined below.

Root Cause	Action you can take to resolve the conflict
Your hostility towards another person due to their success	You may feel angry towards someone because they have achieved success and you have not. Bear in mind that you can't turn the clock back and change things. You can't take their success away, and even if you try, you probably won't spoil it for them. Look for ways in which you can benefit from their success and, instead of wasting time and energy getting mad, direct that same time and energy towards getting better. Even if, in your opinion, they don't deserve their success, they did not succeed just to make you feel bad. They did it for themselves. Now you must do it for yourself.
Someone else's hostility towards you due to your success	Their hostility and anger will arise out of disappointment, bitterness, jealousy, shattered dreams … whatever. If you respond by being angry, then you will definitely make

Root Cause	Action you can take to resolve the conflict
	matters worse. Try to re-establish a sound working relationship by adopting, whenever possible, a win/win approach. Support them in their own efforts to win success, and recognize their achievements. If this is not possible (for whatever reason), distance yourself. Practise your assertiveness skills and, no matter what happens, remain utterly professional in all your dealings with this person. Do not, under any circumstances, attempt to retaliate or adopt an I win/You lose approach.
Your hostility towards another person due to their objectives and beliefs	Your hostility will not change what they believe, but it will cause conflict and bad feeling. Agree to disagree, and respect their right to think and feel in whatever way they choose. Remember that if you disagree with some one's objectives or beliefs, you have the **right** to do that. Equally, they have the **right** to hold those objectives and beliefs.
Someone else's hostility towards you due to your objectives and beliefs	Even if someone is angry towards you, or behaving badly because your objectives and beliefs are different to theirs, do remember that you have the **right** to think and feel however you choose. They also have the **right** to disagree with you, and think and feel in different ways. Look for the areas of common agreement and build on those.
Your hostility towards another person due to their invasion of your territory	The key point is that the other person may have no idea that you are so upset because they have used your office, taken your secretary's time, been given a better computer than you … or whatever. These things may be totally unimportant and irrelevant to them, and they will not have any idea of the depth of your irritation or anger. You may want to explain, assertively, that you don't want this to happen again, e.g.: 'By the way, Mike, I'd prefer it if you didn't use my computer when I'm not in the office because I have it configured in a certain way, and I like it to be left like that.'
Someone else's hostility towards you due to your invasion of their territory	Some people are very territorial about certain, specific things which may not be important to you. If the core of the conflict is about territory, recognize that the chair, the job title, the 'special working relationship' or what ever may be terribly, terribly important to the other person. Don't get angry - just recognize the importance to the other person of the territory which is involved.
Your hostility towards another person due to irrational hostility	If you find yourself feeling hostile to someone without a **logical** reason or cause, then the root of the hostility is likely to be **irrational hostility**. Maybe you've objected because they talk loudly, or because they wear 'bad taste' clothes, or because they have an irritating laugh, or remind you of someone you once disliked in the past. When

Root Cause	Action you can take to resolve the conflict
	irrational hostility strikes, take some time to reflect on why this has occurred. Look beyond the immediate surface cause (the voice, laugh, clothes), and look for the real person. The factor which irritates you may well be a smokescreen the person is using to hide a lack of confidence, or even a desire to impress you.
Someone else's hostility towards you because of irrational hostility	If someone is behaving in a hostile way towards you and you recognize that this is due to an **irrational hostility**, then there is not too much you can do. You have the right to be yourself, and if this person doesn't approve of some aspect of you – e.g. the car you drive, the sport you discuss, the way your mind works, etc. – then that is how it is. If you feel it is appropriate, look for some common interest or objective which may help this person to view you in a difference light. Otherwise, behave cordially and keep a professional distance.
Your hostility towards another person because of their personal style	Begin by recognizing that the other person has the **right** to operate according to their personal style. So if they jump in and make, in your view, rash decisions, then you have to accept that that is their style. If they talk incessantly and are forever out and about, seeing people and doing things, then that is their style. Focus on common objectives, and accept that their way of achieving those objectives may be very different to yours, but may be equally as effective.
Someone else's hostility towards you because of your personal style	Your personal style is an amalgamation of the way you communicate, think and behave. Although it may be different to someone else's personal style, it is how you are – and you have the **right** to be yourself. Demonstrate that, even if your style is different, you are working towards the same objectives and you share a common interest in achieving those objectives successfully.

CASE STUDY 2

In Case Study 2 you are being invited to take action by someone else, on their behalf. The comments made by Josie may be an accurate reflection of the situation, or they may be her perception of the situation. In these circumstances, strategies to **avoid** include the following:

Blaming

Even though the information you are given may come from a well-respected member of the team, make sure that you have all the facts before you involve anyone else. Don't jump in at the deep end and start apportioning blame.

Ignoring

Don't be tempted to walk away and let the people involved just get on with it. The signs of conflict are clear and, if left, the situation could rapidly escalate from a minor issue to a major problem.

Bullying

Don't be tempted to call the people involved into your office, 'read them the riot act' and tell them to get on with their jobs. Bullying tactics will not help you to get to the core of the problem, and will be neither helpful nor useful.

Strategies to **use** include the following:

Checking the facts

Once you have been given information your first task is to check, for yourself, the truth of the allegations. Don't take anyone else's word. Find out the facts and, if you are completely satisfied that there is no case to answer, you need to speak to the person who brought you the incorrect information in the first place. Point out that: (a) you have personally investigated the matter and have not discovered any problems; (b) this kind of behaviour is unacceptable and is not to be repeated.

Intervening

This is necessary if you sense that there **may** be some truth in the allegations, **or** if you feel that there is a genuine breakdown in working relationships between the people involved. You will need to confront both people and get to the heart of the matter.

The intervention process involves the five steps shown in Figure 6.3 below.

Figure 6.3 The intervention process

- **Step 1** – Intervene
  Where conflict exists, it is important to let the people involved know that you know what is going on, and that you intend to take positive action to deal with the problem.

- **Step 2** – Listen and discuss
  Get everyone involved together, sit them down and listen to **all** sides of the story. Give equal time and attention to everyone and ask questions. Make sure you understand (a) the facts and (b) the perceptions. You can guarantee that, where conflict exists, each person involved will perceive the situation in a different way:

  'It's his fault because …'

  'That's absolute nonsense! It's her fault because …'

  By allowing each person to give his or her views and opinions you will have the chance to hear what each person thinks, and he or she will have the chance to hear what the others involved think, too. This can often be very enlightening for people involved in a conflict situation. No matter what happens, keep calm and remain assertive. Your role is to remain impartial throughout, so don't take sides, give an opinion or allow yourself to become involved in the situation.

- **Step 3** – Make your position clear
  Be uncompromising about the fact that you want the situation resolved. By all means show that you want a win/win outcome, but take a tough stand and let everyone know that you will not tolerate behaviour or attitudes which are detrimental to the organization, the department or the team.

- **Step 4** – Negotiate a win/win outcome
  At this stage you are looking for a resolution which is acceptable to everyone. Ask the people involved to say what they would like to see happen. Returning to the situation in Case Study 2, an example of how this might work would be:

  Manager: 'So, it seems to me that what Nicholas is saying is that the data is inaccurate because you're asking for the figures before he has time to correlate all the statistics. Is that right, Nicholas?'

  Nicholas: 'That's exactly right!'

  Manager: 'So, Josie, is there a way around this?'

  Josie: 'Well no, not really … I have to get the figures from Nicholas on the 25th because Tom wants them on the 26th, and that's all there is to it!'

  Manager: 'Nicholas, what's the latest date for you to gather all the information?'

Nicholas: 'I can't do it before the 26th because I don't get the figures from Barnsley until then.'

Manager: 'So what would be a solution from your point of view?'

Nicholas: 'More time!'

Manager: 'So it seems to me that if you, Nicholas, can get the figures from Barnsley earlier, or you, Josie, can give the figures to Tom later, then we could resolve the problem. Does that make sense?'

Nicholas: 'Well yes …'

Josie: 'Yes – but Tom won't be happy about that!'

Manager: 'Have you asked him?'

Josie: 'Well, no … not exactly …'

Move slowly towards a solution which the conflicting parties will find acceptable. This may involve a measure of compromise, but look for the win/win. Do not attempt to impose a solution – it won't work because the people in conflict won't want it to work. It may be frustrating, and it will almost certainly be time-consuming, but, if you invest time at the start, you will save time later on. Remember, little upsets can grow into major battles if left unattended. Before the meeting ends, make sure that everyone concerned is crystal clear about the agreements which have been made. Leave no room for 'Oh, I didn't understand' or 'I didn't think **I** was supposed to be doing that.' For example:

'OK, so what we've agreed is that Nicholas will ask Barnsley to send the figures on the Internet on the 24th. Josie will explain the situation to Tom and ask if she can submit the figures on the 26th, in the afternoon. Nicholas, you'll work on the data on the 24th and 25th, and Josie, you will prepare the report on the 25th and 26th and submit the final document on the 26th. Are we agreed?'

Do bear in mind that even the most highly intelligent, qualified and experienced people can lose all sense of reason because of:

- success as a source of conflict
- objectives and beliefs as a source of conflict
- territory as a source of conflict
- irrational hostility as a source of conflict
- personal style as a source of conflict.

Your role is to provide a *voice of reason*, help people to reach working agreements and then make sure those agreements stick.

■ **Step 5** – Monitor the situation

Unfortunately, you can't just walk away and wash your hands of the whole affair, however much you might like to. Following on from your intervention, you should monitor the situation carefully. You can do this, both formally and informally, through:

– a formal follow-up meeting (or even a series of meetings), attended by all interested parties
– informal meetings (management by walking about) just to check how things are going.

If things are working out, you can breathe a sigh of relief and move on. If the conflict has not been totally resolved, then you will need to go back to step 1, intervention, and start the process all over again.

CASE STUDY 3

In Case Study 3 your CEO has asked you to talk to people and 'get them to see sense' or, put another way, 'Get them to agree to do something they don't seem to want to do'. In this situation, strategies to **avoid** include the following:

Appeasing

Don't, **ever**, be tempted to make promises you can't keep, or embellish the truth to turn a situation around. This, when your strategy comes to light, will just make matters worse. You will lose trust and credibility because of your unethical and unprofessional behaviour.

Divide and rule

This is a slightly different version of appeasement, and involves giving different stories to different people, or maybe offering different inducements to get the desired end result.

Imposing

This strategy involves going in to the situation with 'all guns blazing' and laying down the law: 'This is how it is, and this is how it's going to be. Anyone who doesn't like it can leave now.' People may be stunned into silence by this approach, but you will simply drive the conflict underground and encourage further, and possibly more destructive, conflict.

Strategies to **use** include:

■ listening and discussing
■ giving due consideration to people's concerns
■ negotiating and compromising

- working towards a win/win outcome
- allowing people to take ownership of the solution.

Knocking heads together, giving in or imposing the law does nothing to solve conflict. But if you help people to reach a solution they feel comfortable with, they will take ownership of the solution and want to make it work. There is no specific formula for this, because every situation is different. The keys to success are communication, assertiveness and patience. Don't lose your temper and click into aggressive mode. Don't allow aggressive behaviour to push you into being non-assertive. Use the list shown in Figure 6.4 as a checklist to remind you of the key actions to take.

- Listen carefully
- Ask questions and keep on asking until you are sure you understand
- Use open body language
- Use 'I' and 'My' statements
- State your opinions, say what you would like to see happening
- Give everyone else the chance to have their say
- Move, one step at a time, towards agreement
- Search for a win/win outcome where everyone feels they have achieved something which is of benefit to them
- Keep calm and don't lose your temper
- Think before you speak
- Be consistent, fair and even-handed towards everyone
- Don't give in to bullying tactics
- Remember your rights
- Remember everyone else's rights

Figure 6.4   Assertiveness checklist for conflict resolution

The next activity gives you an opportunity to record your progress in resolving a conflict situation at work.

ACTIVITY 35

1   Briefly describe the cause of the conflict.

2   Who is involved in the conflict?

3   What were their positions at the start of the conflict?

4   What steps did you take to check the facts?

5   When and how did you first intervene?

6   What strategy did you use to resolve the conflict?

7   What agreements were reached between the parties at the end of the first meeting?

8   How did you monitor the situation?

9   Did the agreements hold, or was it necessary for you to intervene again? If so, what happened?

10 What was the final outcome?

11 What did you learn from this?

12 What actions would you repeat in the future in a similar situation?

13 What actions would you avoid in the future in a similar situation?

Learning summary

1 The main root causes of conflict are:
   - success
   - objectives and beliefs
   - territory
   - irrational hostility
   - personal style

2 The main symptoms of conflict are difficulties with communication and deteriorating work standards. The tactics which are most frequently used in a conflict situation are:
   - distorting the facts
   - using metres of 'red tape'
   - bypassing official channels
   - using subtle sabotage

3 Strategies to avoid when seeking to resolve conflict between other people include:
   - blaming
   - ignoring
   - bullying

- appeasement
- divide and rule
- imposing

4 Strategies to use when seeking to resolve conflict between other people include:

- checking the facts
- giving due consideration to people's concerns
- allowing people to take ownership of the solution

5 The five-step intervention process consists of:

1 intervening
2 listening and discussing
3 making your position clear
4 negotiating a win/win outcome
5 monitoring the situation and intervening again, if necessary

6 Strategies to avoid when seeking to resolve conflict between yourself and someone else include:

- confrontation
- collusion or collaboration
- retaliation

7 When you want to resolve conflict between yourself and someone else, you need to determine and deal with the root cause by keeping an open mind and using assertive communication and behaviour.

Information toolbox

Interpersonal skills

Goleman, Daniel (1997) *Working with Emotional Intelligence*, Bloomsbury Publishing plc

Murdock Alex, Scutt Carol (2003) *Personal Effectiveness*, Butterworth Heinemann

Assertiveness

Michelli, Dena (1998), *Successful Assertiveness in a Week*, Institute of Management Foundation, Hodder and Stoughton

Willcocks, Graham & Morris, Steve (1996) *Putting Assertiveness to Work: a programme for management excellence*, Institute of Management Foundation, Pitman

Gillen, Terry (1995), *Positive Influencing Skills*, Institute of Personnel and Development

Stress

Horton, David (2001) *Feel Good Factor: a positive guide to managing unwanted stress*, Peter Honey Publications

ONeill, Liz & ONeill, Brian (2001) *Test Your Stress Resilience*, Institute of Management (IM test yourself series)

Stress Management: self first, Institute of Management Foundation (IM management checklists 034)

Time management

Treacy, Declan (2002) *Time Management in a Week*, Chartered Management Institute, Hodder and Stoughton (CMI business in a week series)

Roberts-Phelps, Graham (1999) *Working Smarter: getting more done with less effect time and stress*, Thorogood

Forsyth, Patrick (2000) *First Things First: how to manage your time for maximum performance*, Institute of Management, Prentice Hall (IM smarter solutions series)

Diversity

Speechley, Chris & Wheatley, Ruth (2001) *Developing a Culture for Diversity in a Week*, Institute of Management, Hodder and Stoughton (IM business in a week series)

Conflict management

Crawley, John & Graham Katherine (2002) *Mediation for Managers: resolving conflict and rebuilding relationships at work*, Nicholas Brealey (People skills for professionals series)

Fox, Anne (2002) *Managing Conflict*, Spiro Press (Fast track series)

Handling conflict situations, Institute of Management Foundation (IM management checklists 046)